1997

(Book 2 in the
90s Flashback Series)

KIRSTY MCMANUS

ISBN: 9781697039351

For all the writers in my awesome community

THANKS TO...

I have an even bigger thank you this time for all the wonderful people who helped me with the second part of this series. Not only did you have a short deadline (due to my not-so-great time management of external events), but you all gave me such insightful feedback that showed you cared about the story and wanted to help to make it the best it could possibly be. Thank you!

Natasha – wow! I can't believe you read it so quickly and were able to give me exactly what I needed! Thank you!

Louise, again, thanks for your take on things. I love how your brain works!

Kate, thank you for reminding me to consider particular storytelling principles! I need those little suggestions every now and again!

Diane, your gentle approach is still very much appreciated. Thank you again for being such a great writing buddy.

Lindsay, I am so glad I got to work with you a second time. I look forward to many more projects together!

Lastly, Sofie, Anna and Belinda. You women are awesome, and I really appreciate the time you take to read my stuff!

ONE

It's been seven months since my life changed forever. Seven months since I burst out of *The Matrix* after living for years and years in total blissful ignorance. Until that point, I thought my life was perfect. I had a handsome husband, a beautiful house, and a great job.

And then BLAM!

A weird psychedelic drug thrust me back into 1996, and I discovered that my husband never loved me as much as he loved someone else.

It came as quite a shock.

Since then, I've been finding it a bit difficult to come to terms with my new reality. Mind you, it hasn't been all bad. I've reconnected with a bunch of old friends, and my relationship with my sister is stronger than ever—but to adjust to being single after an eighteen-year relationship is definitely not what I'd call easy.

"Anna?"

I look up. Kelsey is staring at me.

"Sorry, what?"

"You're off in la-la land again, aren't you?"

"I'm trying really hard not to be."

She sighs. "Well, how about we call it a day and then meet again on Monday? We still have a lot to do."

"I know. Thank you for being so understanding. I'm sorry I'm distracted."

Since Kelsey and I reconciled, we've decided to go into business together. She'd been an event planner at a Shell Beach golf club for a few years but was wanting to go out on her own at some point—and because she knew I was a pastry chef and healthy dessert creator, she thought we'd make the perfect partnership. We are currently in my kitchen discussing our new venture's progress, a sort-of concept café called Naughty or Nice.

"Next week, we need to finalise the menu so we can send it off to the printers. And the builders called this morning to say most of the fit-out will be complete in a couple of days. Have you spoken to Amy?"

My sister offered us her interior design skills to make sure that what we envisioned in our heads looked the same in real life. Initially, I was worried we might not work well together, considering I was basically estranged from her for twenty years, but it's been really easy. And fun. She definitely deserves her reputation as one of the city's best designers. Plus, she's not even charging me for her time, which is a huge bonus.

"I spoke to her yesterday. She's just waiting on a friend of hers to finish constructing the chandelier."

The centrepiece of our whole shop is going to be a massive cascade of bubble-shaped lights hanging at the back of the store.

"Cool. And how are you going with—"

My phone cuts off Kelsey's next question. It's Rachel. Since we reconnected last year, she's also become one of my best friends, but she still lives up at Shell Beach. She recently mentioned wanting to have a weekend in Brisbane, so I've invited her to stay.

Kelsey rolls her eyes. "Go on. Answer it."

I mouth her a *thank you* and pick up my phone.

"Hey!" The sound is slightly muffled, so I assume Rachel is in her car. "I'm about fifteen minutes away. Are you at home?"

"I am. Kelsey and I are just finishing up a business meeting."

"Great! See you soon!"

I hang up and look at Kelsey. "Rachel's almost here, so it's probably a good time to wrap this up anyway. Are you sure you can't come out with us tonight?"

"Sorry, no. I have a date."

"With Ben?" Ben is the latest in a string of toy-boys Kelsey has started seeing. She figures it's a win-win situation, because she doesn't want to settle down with anyone, and they don't usually want to, either. I envy her confidence. I would struggle to get naked in front of a man more than five years my junior.

"Yep."

"That must be getting dangerously close to a serious relationship," I tease.

"I wouldn't call three dates serious. But I do like him. And that body!" She fans herself in an exaggerated fashion.

"Okay, okay. I don't want to know. See you next week?"

"Yes! Have fun with Rachel tonight! And don't do anything I wouldn't do."

"Which is what, exactly?"

"I wouldn't go home alone," she says, eyes twinkling.

I shoot her a look. "Kelsey..."

Kelsey thinks my life would be perfect if only I had someone new in it. But I am definitely not ready for a new relationship. I'm still recovering from a divorce. Not to mention trying to forget a certain other person I met last year.

She holds her hands up in surrender. "What? I'm not hassling you."

"All right." I give her a quick hug and see her out.

I go over to the stereo and choose some old Backstreet Boys tunes to get me in a party mood.

Just as I'm singing along to *Everybody* and getting my nineties dance groove on, my phone rings again.

It's Mum.

"Hey, Mum! How are you?"

"Good. Great, actually. I've been trying a bunch of new strategies in an attempt to treat this damn fatigue, and they're sort of working. Finally."

"Oh, that's amazing! I'm so glad you're feeling better." Mum has been battling myalgic encephalomyelitis, otherwise known as chronic fatigue syndrome, for almost two decades now.

"Thanks, honey. I know it's early days, and I don't expect a miracle cure, but I've actually been able to start doing stuff like walk into town without it wiping me out for the rest of the week."

"Does that mean you might be able to come for a visit soon? Maybe the café opening? We're having a small party on Saturday the twenty-fifth."

"Oh, sweetie, I would love that. I can't promise anything, but I'll do everything in my power to get down there and see you. Amy sent me a couple of photos of the place, and it looks fantastic. I'm so proud of you two girls."

"Thanks, Mum." I start to tear up. I do that a lot lately. I think going through a marriage break-up can make you super emotional, even when stuff unrelated to the break-up happens.

"Anyway, I just wanted to let you know that I've been thinking of you, and I'm looking forward to seeing you again soon."

"I really appreciate it. I'm looking forward to seeing you, too."

I hang up, smiling. Life feels much friendlier these days. Well, apart from my relationship with Ed. And I don't think I could ever be besties with Maddie, even though I'm the one who reintroduced her to my now ex-husband. But I'm grateful for all the other relationships I've re-ignited lately.

I quickly straighten up my apartment in preparation for Rachel's arrival. I currently rent a one-bedroom place on the second floor of an old building in Kangaroo Point. I don't have a view of the river, but I am only a block back from the water.

Just as I'm contemplating getting something to drink, the doorbell rings. I fling open the door and Rachel throws her arms around me.

"It's so good to see you!" she says, obviously very excited about being in the city for the weekend.

I hug her back, laughing. "You, too."

"God, I love Brisbane. I don't know if I could live here full-time, but I certainly appreciate the convenience. Everything in Shell Beach closes at 9pm. I can't believe that's the time we're going to be heading out later!"

"It certainly has its benefits. But then, you do have that gorgeous beach."

"True."

I head through to the kitchen and open the fridge. "Would you like a drink?"

"Yes, please."

I pull out a bottle of Prosecco and pour us two glasses, handing her one.

"To getting back out into the scary social jungle," I say, clinking her drink with mine.

"You're right about the scary part. Even the guys on the coast are hard work. I can't imagine what the city boys are going to be like."

"Well, I'm not planning on meeting anyone tonight. I just want to see what's out there."

"I totally understand. I think even when I meet someone new, I'm going to keep it casual. I like my freedom."

"Me, too. So, we'll be all modern and self-sufficient, just with our hot man on call when we need him?"

She giggles. "Exactly."

We down our drinks, and I let Rachel shower while I get out some crackers and cheese. I refill our glasses and queue a few more nineties songs on the stereo. Except then I start thinking of Kurt—even though I'm pretty sure he would never have listened to Ace of Base or En Vogue.

In this reality, he's taken on the form of a distant celebrity—which I guess he kind of is, producing music for famous DJs in London. I can't even look him up, because he doesn't seem to share the same surname with the cousin currently in my bathroom—and when I googled *Kurt music producer London* there were a lot of results. The ones with photos clearly weren't him, and I wasn't about to start randomly emailing the rest. Besides, what would I say? *Hi, you don't know me, but I've met you multiple times in an alternate reality?*

I also don't want to mess with his life if he's happily settled with someone else. I can't be the Maddie in that relationship.

But I so badly want to ask Rachel if she's heard anything else…maybe that he's broken up with his girlfriend and is moving back to Australia? Except I don't want her thinking I'm only friends with her again so I can grill her about him. In her version of reality, I've never met the guy. I already asked too many questions once, and she started to get suspicious. Luckily, she was drunk and hopefully forgot soon after.

No, the best thing to do is try and move on. Kurt isn't real. At least not the version I met. He's just an echo of the past. Who knows what the current incarnation is like? I almost don't want to know. It might be like that time I met a celebrity chef I was kind of obsessed with and he turned out to be a total dick.

I take a large swallow from my refilled glass and wait for Rachel to reappear.

She soon does, wearing a tight pink dress and tall strappy black heels.

"Wow. You look amazing!"

"Thanks, hon. I feel like I should at least dress like I belong in the city."

"You're definitely going to turn heads tonight." I point to her drink. "I got you another one. And feel free to change the music if you're not into Jamiroquai or The Fugees."

"I love this stuff!" She dances around to prove her point. "Go on, get ready so we can catch up properly."

I obey, heading off to the shower.

I have a good feeling about tonight.

TWO

Okay. So, I may have been slightly off about my good feeling. That's not to say it's been bad, per se, just a little…weird.

For a start, Rachel won't let me eat anything. All I've had since lunchtime is the crackers and cheese I made before we left the house. It's now nine thirty, and if I don't have some food soon, I'm going to pass out from the alcohol that feels like it's being pumped directly via IV into my bloodstream.

"Why can't we quickly go across the street and buy a kebab?" I whine. We're currently at the Press Club, and Rachel keeps looking around like she's expecting someone. She also keeps checking her phone every five seconds.

"Because I said."

"That's not a reason!"

"Just trust me. I have a surprise for you tonight."

I narrow my eyes at her. "Wait, what? What kind of surprise?"

"Nothing bad. I promise it'll be super fun."

"Why didn't you tell me this earlier?"

"Because I wasn't sure if it would work out earlier."

"When will you tell me what it is? I assume it involves food?"

"You'll find out in a few minutes."

I suddenly feel uneasy—like I've been ambushed. Rachel isn't as unpredictable as Kelsey—if Kelsey just said the same thing Rachel did, I'd be heading home right now—but I don't like surprises, period. Maybe it's a hangover from last year, when I discovered my husband had a whole secret past I never knew about.

"Can you at least give me a clue?"

"Fine. Yes, it involves food."

"You're acting like you're waiting for someone."

"Just be patient."

I restlessly sip my salted caramel espresso martini and try to calm the nerves bubbling in my stomach. I'm not happy about this at all.

Rachel's phone beeps, and she jumps. I watch as she quickly opens the message. After reading whatever it says, she looks up at me.

"Damn. Slight change of plans. But it's okay. We'll leave in a few minutes."

"And go where?"

"Just across to Wickham Street. All will be revealed there."

"You promise I won't hate whatever it is we're doing?"

"I swear."

"Okay." I don't know if I trust her, but at least I'll be getting food soon. I finish my martini and order one more. Something tells me I'm going to need it.

But by the time the bartender finishes making it, Rachel is standing up. "We have to go now."

"What about my drink?"

"Either leave it or chug it."

I look at the glass. I'm not sure I'll be able to walk if I drink it fast, but I hate wasting money. And alcohol. I pick it up and swallow the whole thing in a few mouthfuls.

Rachel laughs. "Maybe now you'll finally relax."

I grab onto her arm and follow her outside. I am definitely in drunk territory now.

"I'm so glad you're visiting," I hiccup. "Even if you're springing a surprise on me."

"It's good to see you too, babe."

A couple of minutes later, we stop outside a furniture design business.

"If you were hoping to do some late-night shopping, I hate to disappoint you, but everything's closed," I joke.

"Ha-ha. No, we're going upstairs." She points to a staircase beside the furniture store entrance.

I look around as we start walking up to the second floor, but I can't figure out what's going on.

And then we get to the top.

Ah.

We're at a restaurant.

A *dark dining* restaurant. Meaning, you have to eat everything in the absence of light.

"You booked us in here?" I can barely walk in a straight line with the lights on. How am I going to manage in the dark?

I look around the foyer, which I assume is preparing us for the upcoming experience with its dim lighting and black curtains. An ominous-looking door is set into the back wall.

"Yup! Don't you think it looks great? I know heaps of people up on the coast who have come down for the weekend just to go here, and they've raved about it."

"I don't know, Rachel…"

"Come on. It'll be fun. Just give it a chance."

"Have you seen the menu yet?"

"Nope! That's half the surprise. You won't know what you're eating until you're in there."

"Hmm…"

"Come on, Anna! I thought this kind of thing would be right up your alley. You're such a foodie."

"I am!" My brain is scrambled. A very far away thought from non-drunk Anna reminds me that I have never been interested in this kind of place, because it turns the food into a gimmick and allows for sub-standard cooking. But I am starving.

"Just give it a chance," she pleads. She stops a passing waitress who has a tray of champagne glasses and grabs one. She then gestures between me and the tray. I shake my head.

"Have you already paid?" I ask.

"Yes. But you can pay me back later. Or not at all. I don't mind."

"Of course I'm going to pay my share. I just wish you'd given me some advance warning." I look around and notice something strange. "Rachel? Why aren't there any men here?"

She inspects the women around us. "I don't know. I guess that's a little weird, huh?"

"Do you think maybe you booked us in on a lesbian night or something?"

She laughs. "I don't think so. I'm sure they would have said when I made the booking. Besides…"

We're interrupted by a tall blonde woman who claps her hands together. "Excuse me, ladies. We're about to go in. My name is Delilah, and I'll be your hostess for the evening. If you haven't done so already, please go and check your bags and phones in the cloakroom. After that, I'd like you to form a conga line for safety. Put your arm on the woman's shoulder in front of you, and we'll head inside, single file."

I watch as some of the women race to the front of the room to start the line. Delilah keeps talking.

"It can be a little unsettling at first but try to relax. I will help you find your seat, but from then on, it's up to you to navigate the space unless there's a scheduled activity. It should go without saying that it's best to take it slow. Don't make any sudden moves. But the most important thing is to have fun!"

Hang on. What did she mean by 'scheduled activity?'

Rachel and I drop off our purses. "What do you think a scheduled activity is?" I ask Rachel.

"I don't know. Maybe bathroom breaks?"

"Then why didn't she just say that?"

"Stop overthinking it! It's going to be fun!"

I take a deep breath and join the line behind Rachel as we shuffle into the darkness.

Wow. This truly is proper inky blackness. My bedroom at home has a window with a street-light outside, so even with heavy blinds, it's never completely dark at night. In here, they have the light equivalent of a pressure lock on a spaceship that we have to pass through to get to the dining area. I'm reminded of the walk-in animal enclosures at the zoo that have double gates designed to stop any of the creatures escaping. I have to be honest. I know how the animals feel.

Delilah explains that she's going to seat us one at a time. Rachel disappears from in front of me, and I hear her saying something to Delilah, but I can't quite make out the words.

A few seconds later, a hand gently clamps down on my forearm and pulls me into one of the corners.

"How do you not fall over anything?" I ask. "Do you have the whole room layout memorised beforehand?"

"Oh, no. I'm not that clever. I'm wearing night-vision glasses."

I don't know how I feel about that.

"Here we are," Delilah says, pushing me down into a chair. It's soft, and something, presumably the tablecloth, tickles my thighs.

"There's wine on the table in front of you," Delilah instructs. "Help yourself, but just a tip: tuck your finger over the edge of the glass so you can tell when it's full. You don't want to end up with a lap full of alcohol."

Rachel laughs. "Too late."

I feel around on the table and locate a plate, some cutlery, a water glass, and a wine glass.

"I'm glad you wore that J'Adore perfume," Rachel jokes. "I'll be able to sniff you out if we get separated."

"I guess the same goes for you," I say. "Since I don't think I've ever met anyone else who wears that fragrance you've insisted on wearing every day since high school."

"Hey, it's my thing. And I get a lot of compliments, thank you very much."

Rachel wears Opium by Yves Saint Laurent. And yes, it's a lovely perfume, but it also reminds me of my great aunt Frieda. Rachel may as well have chosen 4711 as her signature scent. That fragrance has been around since 1799!

I pour myself some wine as per Delilah's instructions. I was hoping to eat something before I ingested more alcohol, but the dark is messing with my head. "I wonder who we'll end up sitting next to. If this isn't a lesbian night, maybe it's a bunch of bachelorette parties."

"Can I tell you something?"

"It depends what it is."

"Please don't get mad, but I kind of invited two people along."

"You what? Who? Do I know them?"

"No. It's two guys…"

I reach out into the darkness and find Rachel's arm to slap it. Not hard, but just enough so she knows how annoyed I am.

"How could you? Not only did you spring this dark dining thing on me, but you also invited two literal blind dates?"

"They're not blind dates. *I* know who they are…"

I cut her off. "I don't care. You shouldn't have tricked me like this."

"I wasn't trying to trick you. And it's not what you're thinking…"

"Then tell me, what am I thinking, and how is it different?"

"They were running late. I was going to introduce you to them before when we were at the Press Club, but one of them got held up, so they said they'd meet us here. I promise there's no pressure on you to do anything."

"They better *not* have any expectations from tonight."

"I just said they won't. It was only supposed to be a bit of fun. One of the guys is…"

"Okay, ladies!" Delilah's voice comes over a PA system. "I trust you're all settled in and have found the wine. We'll be serving the appetisers soon, but first, we'll start with a little icebreaker. Pete, will you please bring the gentlemen in and line them up against the wall?"

The women start whooping and cheering.

"What's going on?" I ask, alarmed.

"I don't know," Rachel says, sounding genuinely confused. "I swear I didn't know there was going to be anything like this."

I reach across to the seat next to me, but it's empty. I slide into it and feel in the darkness to see if there's anyone in the next one along.

"Ow!" a giggly female voice squeaks. "Careful! You just poked me in the eye!"

"Sorry. Um, do you know what's happening?"

"What do you mean?"

"This icebreaker thing. What's going on?"

"I guess it's the first blind speed-dating activity."

"The *what?*" I'm going to kill Rachel. "Rachel? Did you know this is a *blind speed-dating* event?"

"No, I didn't! I promise. Holy shit…"

I slide back into my own chair and hiss at her. "I can't believe you did this! We have to leave now."

She grabs my shoulder in the dark, showing a surprising sense of direction. "No, please. We have to stay. The guys I invited will freak out if they find out we're not here."

"Well, we'll get Delilah to tell them we'll meet them outside."

"Okay. But don't leave without me."

"Excuse me?" I call out in the darkness. "Delilah? Waiter? Anyone?"

Delilah's voice is soon beside us. "Yes, ladies? Is there a problem?"

"Uh, sort of. We didn't know the evening would include these kinds of activities."

"You didn't?" she says, sounding incredulous. "But this is a blind speed-dating event. What did you expect?"

"There's been a bit of a misunderstanding. My friend here apparently didn't read the fine print when she made the booking."

"But you would have filled out all the paperwork explaining everything already, including a waiver agreeing to follow all instructions once you entered the restaurant."

"I didn't do any such thing!" I say.

"It was all in the info pack," she explains. "Along with the stuff to say you wouldn't sue us if you fall over in the dark and hurt yourself."

"Rachel," I demand. "Did you sign something on my behalf?"

"Um, I did sign an indemnity thing. Sorry, I had to. It was the only way I could make this a surprise, but I definitely did not read anything about speed-dating. Uh, Delilah? Will you be able to seat the guys I invited at our table after this first round?"

"Of course."

"Great." Rachel finds one of my hands and holds it between both of hers. "Can we just do the first activity, and then we'll all leave together? I'm sure it won't be that bad."

"Delilah? What does this first activity involve?" I ask.

"Oh, it's just a little harmless fun. Hang on. I was about to explain it to everyone." Her voice echoes around the room again. "For those new to blind speed-dating, I'll explain how our first activity works. It's called *Guess That Man*. The gentlemen are now lined up next to each other against the back wall, and the women will be guided down the line and encouraged to get to know each one by touching their face. No words will be exchanged, but if a woman likes the feel of any of the men, she can raise her hand and our staff will make a note of it. Then we'll swap over. At the end, we'll pair up any potential matches."

A series of appreciated "woos" go around the room.

"Nope," I say to Rachel.

"We do have a couple of rules to ensure the safety of our guests," Delilah continues. "Touching below the neck is prohibited. This is non-negotiable. Our staff are wearing night-vision glasses, and we will see if you're not doing the right thing. A breach will result in you being escorted off the premises immediately. And secondly, while I know this sounds a little sexist, only women are allowed to initiate kisses, and even then, there's no obligation. Of course, gentlemen, you are allowed to reject an unwanted advance, and if you feel uncomfortable at any time, raise your hand, and someone will come over to assist you. We want this to be fun, but also consensual for all those involved."

"Come on," Rachel begs. "You barely have to do anything. Technically, all you have to do is stand there, or maybe tweak a guy's nose to let him know there's someone standing in front of him. It'll all be over in a few minutes and then we can get the guys and leave."

A feeling of dread mixed with morbid curiosity settles in my chest. Something tells me it's not going to be that simple.

"I'll give it ten minutes, and then I'm leaving," I say finally. "And if any of those guys break the rules, I'm outta here, no warning. I may also decide to leave before we swap. I don't want a bunch of random men pawing at my face."

"Okay," she says, sounding relieved. "Believe me, this isn't how I expected to be spending my night, either. I can't imagine what my guys are going to think, being lined up against the wall and felt up."

"So, we're all good, ladies?" Delilah asks.

"I wouldn't exactly say we're good, but yes, we're as ready as we'll ever be." I sigh.

"Excellent." She grabs my arm and pulls me across the room.

I feel a little sick.

What on earth have I just agreed to?

THREE

The anticipation is killing me. Not to mention how increasingly difficult it is to stay upright. That last bit of wine was not the smartest idea I've had.

Delilah has placed me back in another conga line, and I'm reluctantly waiting my turn to get to know the guys. "Here's your first victim," Delilah tells me, taking my hands and planting them directly on someone's face.

"Oh, sorry," I say. "That couldn't have been very comfortable."

The guy chuckles. He sounds pretty normal, which is reassuring.

"No talking!" Delilah admonishes.

I take a deep breath and lean in a little, gently feeling my way around the guy's face. I think he's smiling. His jaw is slightly rough, like he shaved this morning, and it's already grown back a bit. His ears are soft. No earrings. I make my way over his eyebrows. Is that a normal amount of bushiness? I have no idea. And then I feel his hair. It has some sort of product in it and feels like it's spiked up. His aftershave is a little strong, but not too bad.

Hmm. What now? Are we really supposed to want to kiss these guys after a couple of moments touching their faces? While this one seems nice enough, I'm definitely not motivated to kiss him. But it's not as bad as I expected. In fact, it's almost entertaining, in a car-crash TV sort of way. But then, it's highly likely the alcohol in my system has reached a point where I find everything funny and interesting.

"Time to move along," Delilah barks.

I move up to the next guy. He seems nervous and jerks at my touch. He also smells a little sweaty. I try to be polite and gently feel my way along his neck to his head. He lets out a hissy giggle, a bit like Ernie from *Sesame Street*.

Wow. That's a lot of hair. And it goes so high!

"Next!" calls Delilah. I'm grateful these interludes are short. I wonder how many women are putting up their hands or going in for kisses.

I slowly reach my hands out for the next guy. I'm sort of getting into the spirit of the activity now, and I start by slowly running a finger along his Adam's apple, up to his chin. He has a little scruff on the lower half of his face. I use both hands to explore his cheeks and temples. Above his eyebrow is something a little bumpy. Maybe scar tissue?

His hair feels wavy and stops just above his collar. I run my fingers through it. It feels nice.

I'm shocked to find something stirring in me. How is it possible I'm attracted to a total stranger, just from stroking his face?

"Thank you, ladies. Please move on to your next man."

Oh.

I surprise myself by being disappointed. Before I move on, I press my index finger to his lips. He kisses it, and the sensation reverberates all the way through my body.

Whoa.

I half-heartedly participate in the rest of the round, but none of the other guys even come close to evoking the same feelings as Mystery Man Number Three.

"All right! Now we're going to swap over. Remember, no talking! And the ladies are still in charge of kisses."

Originally, I was going to pull out of this round, but I can't help myself.

I need to make contact with that guy again.

Delilah positions me against the wall, and I wait nervously for the first person to come along.

Ugh. This guy's hands are calloused, and he pulls at my face as if he's moulding a lump of clay. I reach up and slap him away.

"Sorry," he whispers. "I have no idea what I'm doing."

Clearly. But I don't say that out loud.

The second guy is definitely the sweaty guy. His hands are clammy and unskilful, and I know he has to be the one with the big hair.

I hold my breath for Guy Number Three.

I sense as he leans in and starts tugging at my nose and ears. No. That couldn't be him, surely?

The fourth, fifth and sixth guys are forgettable. I'm starting to wonder if I just imagined that initial connection.

Several more guys take their turn before Delilah pipes up. "All right, people. This is the last one. Make it count!"

I wait.

Someone steps forward, and I feel one of his fingers trace my temple down to my neck. I shiver. His hands gently stroke all the contours of my face, under my eyes, beside my nose, and over my lips.

Oh my God. This is better than sex. Although, I'm not exactly an expert on that these days.

He reaches forward and caresses the back of my neck.

As if I'm under a spell, I lean forward and find his lips with mine in the dark. They are warm and soft, and somehow perfect. It doesn't seem strange at all that I'm kissing a literal stranger. Right now, it feels like I've known him forever. But I am fully aware it could also be the alcohol and darkness playing tricks on me.

I don't care if I'm breaking the rules as I run my own hands along his neck and face. I feel that scruff and wavy hair from the last round, which confirms it's definitely the same guy I connected with before.

"I'm afraid time's up, everyone," Delilah calls out. "But rest assured, we'll make sure all matches are notified by the end of the evening."

Oh, I forgot to put my hand up!

Delilah guides me back to my seat. "Can you please make sure my name is put down next to that last guy?" I ask her.

She laughs. "Ah. It wasn't as bad as you expected, huh?"

"No, it wasn't," I admit contritely.

"Sure, hon. I'll write your name down next to Mr. Hot Stuff."

I remember that she's wearing night-vision glasses and I want to ask her what my guy looks like, but she disappears before I get the chance.

"Are you there, Rachel?" I call out.

"Yep. God, I need a *lot* more wine after that. Talk about traumatic."

"Really? You didn't enjoy it?"

"Hell, no! Did you?"

"Uh, actually, it wasn't too bad," I say sheepishly.

She squeals. "Don't tell me you matched with someone!"

"I may have. Well, only if he put his hand up."

"Ha! And here you were giving me a hard time for bringing you in the first place! I expect a huge apology later."

"You can have one now. I'm sorry. So very, very sorry."

"Wouldn't it be funny if…"

"Ladies? I have one of the two gentlemen from your booking."

"Oh, good," Rachel says. "Billy? Is that you?"

"It is!"

"Great! Take a seat and say hello to Anna. You've already met her face. Here, you can have my spot."

I hear some shuffling around while I assume Billy sits down between us.

"Hi," I say shyly. There's a one in twelve chance this is my guy.

"The other gentleman just had to step out for a moment to take a phone call, but I'll bring him over when he's done," Delilah explains.

"Thank you!" Rachel chirps. "Oh my God, Billy. I'm so sorry about all of this. If I had known it was going to be a speed-dating thing, I would never have suggested it..."

He laughs. "Actually, I had a blast. To be honest, I was kind of relieved when I found out what we were doing. When you first contacted me, I thought you were asking me on a date."

"Oh, really? That's funny," Rachel says weakly.

Uh-oh. I'm guessing that's not what she wanted to hear. I can't even ask her if she's okay, because Billy is sitting between us.

"Did you, um, put your hand up for anyone?" she asks him.

"Yeah, a couple. There was this one chick I kissed, and holy shit..."

No. There is no way I could have kissed Rachel's crush, is there?

"Hey, wouldn't it be weird if it was Anna?" Rachel says, faking enthusiasm.

"Maybe we should find out. Anna, where's your face?"

"Um, I have to go to the bathroom. Rachel?"

"Oh, yeah. I need to go, too. We'll be back in a minute, Billy."

"Sure," he says easily.

I stand up and find Rachel in the dark. We stumble our way through the room and wait for someone to guide us towards the exit.

A waiter opens the door, and we sneak through. Out in the lobby, I blink, readjusting to the light. The bathroom is to our left, so we head in that direction. Once inside, I turn to Rachel.

"Okay, so what's going on? Is Billy someone you were hoping to hook up with?"

She nods miserably. "And now he likes you!"

"No, he doesn't. He likes some other woman he kissed. I didn't kiss him."

"How do you know? Unless you didn't kiss anyone. What about that guy you mentioned?"

I blush.

Her eyes widen. "So, you *did* kiss someone! I knew it. It would be Billy for sure."

"Hang on. Let's not jump to conclusions. What does Billy look like?"

"Uh, he has blue eyes…"

"I mean what does he look like in a way I can confirm?"

"Oh, right. He has a bit of scruff on his face…"

My stomach drops. Not a good start.

"Half the guys had scruff. What else?"

"He's tall. And he has these totally kissable lips…"

Oh no.

"What kind of hair does he have?"

"It's…oh, you know like Josh in *Younger*?"

"You mean short on the sides, but long on the top and combed back with lots of product?"

"Yes! Shit! It *was* him, wasn't it?"

"No! It wasn't! My guy had wavy shoulder-length hair."

Her shoulders sag in relief. And then her eyes light up with recognition. Hang on…don't tell me you kissed…"

The door bursts open, and a woman comes in.

"Excuse me? Is one of you Anna?"

I put up my hand. "Yes?"

"There's a guy outside wanting to talk to you."

Rachel looks at me, grinning. "Go on. It sounds like your match is waiting. I'll be out in a moment."

My heart starts hammering. How did he know who I was? Did Delilah already tell him?

I check my reflection in the mirror. I look terrified, but otherwise okay.

"Wish me luck," I say, hesitantly walking to the door.

"You don't need luck!" she sing-songs before heading to a stall. She looks way too excited by this whole exchange. What is going on with her?

I open the door and walk through.

A guy with Josh hair is standing there, but he's nowhere near as cute as the guy he shares the style with. "Anna?" he asks expectantly.

"Billy?" I confirm.

"Yep. I knew it! You sounded hot in the dark. I couldn't wait any longer to find out."

"Oh. I'm not one of your matches, though."

"How do you know unless we kiss to check?" he says, walking towards me like a predatory tiger.

I step backwards, trying to put some space between us. This is all wrong.

"I just know. And out of respect to Rachel, I'd rather not pursue this any further," I say.

"Pfft. Rachel doesn't care. She brought me to this event! She *wants* me to hook up with other women!"

"Uh, no…I don't think…"

He closes the gap between us. My back hits the wall, and I try to scoot sideways, but he plants a hand either side of me and leans forward.

"Get away!" I yell.

"Just one kiss…" he says, like he's trying to hypnotise me.

"No!" I say firmly. I'm about to scream when he pushes his mouth on mine. I go rigid with shock. Our teeth clash, and I pull my head back, cracking it on the wall.

A jagged pain reverberates around my brain. Billy seems to take this opportunity to double down on his efforts.

I want to throw up.

"Anna?"

I have never been so glad to hear Rachel's voice in my life.

Billy is distracted enough that I can finally push him off me. He shoots me a lazy smile before focusing on Rachel. "Anna and I were just having a little fun, weren't we?"

"No. We were not," I say adamantly.

"What's going on?" Rachel asks, confused.

"Nothing is going on." I look down at my hands and see they're shaking. "I want to go home," I tell her.

"Come on, the night's just getting started," Billy says, still with that sleazy grin on his face.

"Were you just kissing Billy?" Rachel asks.

"He kissed *me*," I correct. "Without permission."

"It didn't feel like that to me," he says.

"You're disgusting," I say and stomp off. "Rachel, you can do what you want, but I'm leaving now."

She looks from me to Billy and back again.

"I..."

"It's fine. Go back in. I'll see you later."

"Anna..."

I don't stay to hear what she has to say. She clearly isn't prepared to leave immediately, and there's no way in hell I'm going back inside where I'll be at the mercy of that creep.

I hurry out to the cloakroom in the lobby and ask the clerk to retrieve my bag. I then head outside to find a cab to take me home.

It isn't until I'm safely in the back seat of one, heading over the Story Bridge, that I burst into tears.

FOUR

I ignore Rachel's calls and texts for the rest of the night. At one point, I remember she's supposed to be staying at my place, so I text her without reading her messages and tell her she can still stay over if she doesn't have anywhere else to go. I leave a blanket and pillow on the couch and head off to my room.

It almost feels like the night Kelsey and I stopped talking, because some complete douchebag convinced her I did something I didn't. How could Rachel choose Billy over me? He's so gross. At least from the sounds of it, I don't have to worry about him making a move on her. For a minute, I feel bad that she has to deal with him on her own. Until I remember there's another guy with her. Whoever he is. If he's friends with Billy, I'm glad I didn't have to make awkward small talk with him for the rest of the night.

I toss and turn in bed for ages. I haven't experienced such a varied and intense range of emotions for a while. The whole debacle with Billy almost made me forget that I kissed someone else tonight, and it was pretty damn amazing.

In fact, I would even go so far as to say it matched the last kiss I had. With Kurt.

Back in 1996 on that Sunday afternoon at Sizzler.

I smile at the memory. And then every emotion I've suppressed since

July last year comes roaring back with a vengeance. It's probably the late hour and the residual alcohol in my veins, but I need to see him. Now.

I know it isn't real, and I always feel worse afterwards, but I can't give him up. I tried really hard, hiding the compound away, mostly because I wanted to sort out my life in the present—but I can't ignore it any longer.

I memorised Kurt's home phone number after he put it in my mobile the last time we met, and if he's still working at the record store, I'll know where he is for part of the week.

I'm doing it. I'm going back.

I get up and put on my robe. I grab my keys and head down into the communal garage where I have a storeroom at the back of my parking space.

I unlock the door and look around at the mountain of boxes I never unpacked.

Kelsey and I labelled them all, so I start to navigate my way through the crowded space. Before I moved, I'd had two boxes from the bathroom: one with everyday stuff, and one with everything else. I'm looking for the latter.

There it is! I gently place it down on the ground in the middle of the storeroom and look at it.

After a minute, I lean down and work my fingernail under the tape sealing the box before ripping it off. I pull out several bottles of old moisturiser and little miniatures of shampoo and conditioner stolen from hotels.

I really should have just thrown all of this away. I haven't needed any of it since I moved, so I can't imagine I'm going to use much of it in the future.

Where is that compound? It was a regular-sized ointment jar, so not so small that it would be difficult to see in the box.

My heart beats a little faster as I yank out one thing after another without finding it.

When I reach the bottom and have double-checked each item multiple times, I come to a grim realisation.

It's not here.

No! That can't be the end of the story! I refuse to believe that I will never go back to the past or see Kurt again. That jar was still practically full!

I look at my watch. It's after midnight. I can't do anything about it now.

I reluctantly seal the box back up and head upstairs again.

I don't think I'm going to get any more sleep tonight.

***

Apparently my body decided it could sleep after all. I manage to drift off for a few hours at 4am, and then wake up feeling crusty around nine.

Rachel never tried to come back here. I'm not so heartless that I don't worry about her safety, so I reluctantly open my messages to see if she responded to my last one.

There are three from her. Two before I texted and one after. I only read the newest one.

Don't worry. I'll figure something out.

That's it? It's almost as if she's mad at *me* for leaving *her*!

I pick up my phone and call Kelsey. "Hey, it's me."

"Hey. How are you? What happened with you and Rachel last night?"

"Why? What did she say?"

"Not much that I could understand. She called me up around midnight to tell me that she loved me. And she said you were mad at her."

"Pfft. Only because she wouldn't leave after her creep of a friend forced himself on me."

"Oh no. I'm sorry, babe. Do you want to talk about it?"

"Not really."

"Do you know where she is now?"

"Nope. I said she could stay here, but she told me she'd figure something else out. She's obviously not at your place, then?"

"No. Do you think we should be worried?"

"I don't know. Crap. I'll contact her after I hang up."

"Okay. Let me know if you need me to do anything."

"Thanks. Oh, and before I forget, I know this is a long shot, but do you remember when you helped me move, and you packed up my bathroom stuff?"

"Uh, yeah?"

"Do you remember seeing a small jar with a label on it called Youth Compound?"

"I have no idea."

"It was in amber glass with a black-and-white label."

"I'm sorry, babe, but I really don't know. Why?"

"It was a product I got from my sponsor. They're asking me to do a write-up for their internal files, and I need to give them the batch number." I figure that's more believable than trying to explain the truth.

"Again, I'm sorry, but I don't remember if I saw it."

"Never mind. I just thought on the off-chance…"

"Maybe Ed borrowed it," she says cheekily. "And thought he needed a bit of a helping hand. Can I just say now that I never thought he was very hot?"

"Well, I would have been a little worried if you did covet my ex-husband, but I appreciate what you're trying to do. Hmm…I don't think Ed would have taken it, because…"

I was going to say because he'd already moved out the last time I saw the jar, but there was that time I was up in Shell Beach and he came to get some of his stuff. Could he have taken the compound then? But why? He would have known it wasn't his.

"Actually, you might be on to something. I have to go."

"No problem. Bye!"

I hang up. I want to call Ed, but I need to check if Rachel is okay first. I figure I'll send a text and then if she hasn't gotten back to me by the time I've finished talking to Ed, I'll phone.

Did you find somewhere to stay last night?

There.

I quickly dial Ed's number.

"Hello, Ed's phone, Maddie speaking. Is that you, Anna?"

I hate caller ID.

"Uh, yes. Hi. Is Ed there?"

"He's in the shower. Can I take a message?"

"Could you please ask him to check for a product I need to write about for my sponsor? It's called Youth Compound. I think maybe he accidentally packed it into his stuff when he came over just before we sold the house?"

"Oh, he asked me to do that for him. He had to run off to a meeting that day, so I packed up everything in the bathroom I thought was his."

"And you thought the Youth Compound was Ed's?"

"I don't remember, but I suppose it's possible. Ed uses moisturiser on his face, so maybe I thought it belonged to him."

"It's not moisturiser, it's a supplement. It was in an amber glass container with a black-and-white label."

"Um, okay. That means nothing to me."

"Can you go see if it's in your bathroom cabinet?" I'm starting to lose my patience.

"What? Now?"

"Yes, please. I have to account for all the stuff I get from my sponsor. If I lose anything, particularly if it's an unreleased product, I can get in trouble."

I don't know where I came up with that, but it sounded good.

"All right, hang on." I hear her shuffling through the house. "Oh. He's locked the door. He must be…um…"

I want to screech in frustration. "Well, can you please ask him to check as soon as possible and get back to me? It's kind of urgent."

"Will do."

I take a couple of deep breaths. "Thanks, Maddie."

"No problem."

I hang up and pull a face at my reflection in the wardrobe mirror. I need that compound!

I don't know much about drug addiction, but I can imagine this is what a craving feels like. Now that I've got my heart set on seeing Kurt again, I would do almost anything to satisfy my fix.

My phone beeps. For a second, I assume it's Maddie texting to let me know she found the jar already, but it's just Rachel.

Yeah. It was fine. I'll drop by and pick up my stuff from your place later.

I stare at the message. No *I'm sorry my douchey friend kissed you without your permission and I stayed with him?*

I can't deal with this right now. I quickly type back.

I have to go out, so I'll drop your stuff at Kelsey's. You can get it from her place later.

All right. Now back to the important business of worrying about the missing compound.

***

I basically do nothing for the rest of the day, which is a bit of a shame, considering it's one of my only days off this week. The one time I leave the house is to drop Rachel's stuff at Kelsey's, and I don't stay to chat. After that, I lock myself in my apartment and watch mindless TV. I can't concentrate on anything else. When Ed calls or texts to let me know he's found the compound, I want to be able to go pick it up straight away.

I'm also feeling a little panicky. What if he found it before today and threw it away, thinking it was junk?

I never followed up with my sponsor to see if anyone at the company knew what it was, but I know for a fact the marketing manager had never heard of it.

If Ed doesn't have it, I might have to follow up with another department. Maybe someone in product development.

I head over to my bookshelf. I put a few of my diaries there when I moved in, but I haven't looked at them since. That should prove I've tried to move on. I really deserve a medal for how much willpower I've displayed.

I pick up the one from the beginning of 1997. I'm assuming if I go back, I'll be returning to the year after, considering it's now the new year here in the present.

I look at the cover fondly, covered in brightly coloured squares featuring illustrated pictures of shells, fish, and flowers. I open up to the first entry and smile at my complaint about New Year's Day being boring because everyone is recovering from the night before.

The whole time I was married to Ed, we never stayed up until midnight. We'd sometimes go to a friend's house or pay for a fancy dinner, but we never stayed awake for the midnight fireworks. Ed couldn't see the point. I wonder if this year he did for Maddie.

Jeez. I have to stop being so bitter. I was the one who got them back together. I need to get over it.

It just feels so unfair, though. He's all happy, and I'm dealing with jerks like Billy.

I skim through the next few pages. It was the school holidays, so I spent most days down at the beach with friends or working at the video store. Kelsey and I were boy-crazy, so we were always on the lookout for cute tourists who were in Shell Beach for the summer. Not that we really dated them, but occasionally we'd agree to meet them at Beans, where we knew Jackson and the other waiters were watching over us.

I'm so glad Jackson is back in my life. Kelsey lives with him now over in the Valley, and we all hang out regularly, along with Jackson's partner, Cash. Both Kelsey and Jackson have helped me through some pretty dark moments in the last few months.

I look at the time. It's after six. That's it. I can't take it anymore. I have to do something.

I grab my handbag and head out the door.

Ed lives with Maddie in Norman Park now, not too far from our old house in Balmoral. Maddie had bought her place a couple of years earlier, but Ed mentioned last time we spoke that he was going to take on half the mortgage.

So, just like that, he's slotted into a brand-new life.

Oops. There I go again.

I probably need to start keeping a gratitude journal or something. I know my life is good. And if I get to see Kurt for a few hours, that should be more than enough to tide me over for the next couple of months.

For a moment, I think about the guy I kissed last night. In the light of day, it seems so bizarre that I did something like that. I've now decided I made a big deal about nothing…it was a single kiss from some random stranger while I was drunk. I'd probably be disappointed if I saw him in person and sober.

I pull up at Ed and Maddie's house and jump out of the car.

I don't stop to think about what I'm doing. All I'm focusing on is that Youth Compound.

I rap on the door a couple of times. After a moment, I hear footsteps in the hallway. The door opens and I let out a small sigh of relief. It's Ed.

He looks slightly taken aback. "Anna! What are you doing here?"

"Did Maddie mention my call this morning?"

"No. What's up?"

I really want to give her the benefit of the doubt, so I refrain from being sarcastic.

"I was looking for a product my sponsor gave me a few months ago. Maddie said she packed up your bathroom stuff that time you came over before I moved."

"Oh, right. Yeah. No, Maddie didn't mention it, but come in. I'll have a look for you."

"Thanks."

"I wouldn't hold my breath, though. I did a big clean-out after I moved in here. Threw out a bunch of old stuff I didn't think I needed anymore."

I swallow the panic rising in my throat. "Let's hope not. I need the batch number for a report I'm writing."

He ushers me down the hall to the bedroom and through a connecting doorway leading to the ensuite. I can't help looking around and comparing my decorating style to Maddie's. Or, I suppose it could be Ed's now, too. Who knows how he's changed in the last few months?

It's a definite contrast to our whites, pale timbers, and neutral colours. I note the rose-coloured wall, the red-toned Turkish rug on the floor, and the ocean-green textured cushions on the tasteful armchair in the corner. It's a look I have always envied when I've entered bohemian-themed furniture stores, yet I have never been brave enough to attempt it on my own.

But then I think of my own apartment, which I have started to be a bit more adventurous with. I wouldn't say I've gone for the same thing as Maddie and Ed, but I've been experimenting more with colour and some cute vintage pieces I found around town. I like that the space is totally mine to do whatever I want with.

Ed rummages in the cupboards. "I don't know what I'm looking for."

"Oh, it's…"

I hear a cleared throat from the doorway. "This looks cosy," Maddie says, looking from Ed to me and back again.

"I…I was just getting that jar I called about this morning," I say.

"Sorry, I ran out of time to ask Ed about it earlier," Maddie says, not sounding like she ever planned on following it up. It's sad, but there's none of the previous warmth I felt from her before she knew who I was. She turns to Ed. "Honey, do you mind checking the lasagne in the oven for me? I'll help Anna."

He looks like he's about to argue but changes his mind. "Sure. I'll, um, talk to you later, Anna."

He hurries off, looking flustered, and Maddie walks over to the bathroom cabinet. "Next time, I'd appreciate you calling ahead before you drop by unannounced."

"But I did call this morning, and you never called back. I really need that product from my sponsor."

"Just tell me what it looks like."

"It's an amber glass container with a white label and black writing."

She sticks her head right inside the cupboard. "I don't think it's…"

My heart starts to sink as she trails off, but then she stands up, holding something in the air. "Is this it?"

"Yes! Oh my God! Thank you! I was worried it might be gone forever."

I hold out my hand so she can give it to me, but she takes her time looking at the label.

"What does it actually do?"

"Oh, it's just a supplement you take to make you feel younger."

"In other words, a waste of money."

"I guess you could say that." Jeez. Talk about a spoilsport. If only she knew that the substance she's holding is responsible for her current domestic bliss.

I reach out and take it out of her hand. "Thanks. I'll leave now."

"I'll show you to the door."

"No need." I hurry out, not even saying goodbye to Ed. Maddie has made it clear she's uncomfortable with me around, and I'm not going to be petty about it.

Besides, I want to have an early night. I have a big day ahead of me tomorrow!

A FEW DAYS EARLIER…

Ed

Happy fucking New Year.

I open my eyes and stare at the ceiling. I still haven't gotten used to this place, and I'm not sure I ever will. Maddie bought it on her own before we reconciled, and it made sense for me to move in at the beginning. There'd already been too much upheaval in our lives to throw a new house into the mix—but if we end up staying together, I'm going to have to insist she sell it. This place is way too girly for my liking.

One of our bedroom walls is pink, for God's sake! Maddie keeps telling me it's called Strawberry Freeze, but that just makes it worse. I can't stand all the pink and red eclectic boho bullshit she's put around the house. A living space should be calm and minimal. A place where you're not assaulted by colours everywhere you look.

I rub my face, which somehow feels both dry and greasy after last night. I can't remember the last time I stayed up until midnight on New Year's Eve, and now I remember why. It's overrated, getting drunk with a bunch of randoms and waiting for the fireworks to go off. What are we? Twelve?

But Maddie wanted to introduce me to some of her friends, so I agreed to go along. I'd managed to avoid most socialising in the last few months, but I couldn't get out of last night.

At the beginning, I made a few allowances so Maddie and I could get reacquainted properly (mostly in the bedroom, if you know what I mean) but then I had to get back to my routine. There were already murmurings around the office that I'd softened…let my game slip. And maybe I had a little. After all, it's not every day you leave a long-term relationship and jump straight back into one with your first love.

I glance over at the woman sleeping beside me. Madeline Mcfeeley. She's still insanely hot—and she's grown into the type of person I knew she'd become all those years ago. But it's definitely been an adjustment.

I'd forgotten how fucking high maintenance she is. She never bloody leaves me alone! I was so used to Anna and I living our own lives that I'd forgotten how time-consuming some relationships can be.

That was one good thing about Anna. She knew her place. But it still stings that she was the one who ended our marriage. I always thought I'd be the one to do it.

I know I wasn't being fair to her, especially at the end, but I couldn't help it. We should never have gotten married in the first place. But after we'd been together for six years, it seemed like I didn't really have a choice. I figured if Anna was okay with the situation, then that was enough.

I think deep down, she always knew I never loved her. And if she didn't, that was her problem. I did my duty as a husband. And I never cheated on her, although God knows I came close dozens of times.

Then one day, I came home from a business trip and BOOM! She dropped the Maddie bombshell.

That was a weird night. I can't remember what I said to Anna, but I know my brain kept blasting these thoughts at me. "You're finally free!" "Holy shit! You're actually going to get a second chance with Maddie!" "I can't believe Anna had the balls to confront you like that!" "You're finally going to be able to have sex with another woman!"

It went on and on like that for a while. Originally, I planned on waiting before I contacted Maddie. I mean, I wanted to give myself some breathing room and enjoy being single for a while, but it didn't happen that way. I ended up walking past her office, just to get an idea of what kind of business she ran (you can tell a lot about a person by their workplace, especially if they're the CEO) and she just happened to be leaving the building at the time. Of course, it was too late to pretend I hadn't seen her, so it all just snowballed from there.

And now I'm stuck.

I'm going to give it six months and then figure out my next move.

Don't get me wrong, I do love Maddie—but I'm a realist. Sometimes that's not enough to keep a relationship going.

I get up, leaving her asleep, and head to the bathroom. I drink a handful of water from the tap and look at my reflection. It's not pretty. My eyes are bloodshot, and I swear there are a bunch of extra lines on my face that weren't there yesterday.

I'm too exhausted to think much about resolutions for the coming year, but I probably need to exercise a little more. Maybe I'll even get some Botox.

I open the cupboard under the sink and rummage around. I wonder if Maddie has any of that anti-aging crap in here.

Right at the back, I find a small amber jar. Bingo.

YOUTH COMPOUND – Wind back the years with our revolutionary formula.
Feel instantly energised!
Dosage: Half a teaspoon dissolved in room temperature water. Effects will last for
approximately twelve hours.
30 doses.

I thought this kind of stuff would normally be in cream form, but I'm not exactly an expert in women's makeup.

I take the jar out to the kitchen and mix up a glass. When the water turns purple and starts bubbling, my resolve falters. But then I remember I'm a guy, and I don't get scared by fizzy coloured water. Besides, Maddie looks great, so if she's taking this, it must work.

I drink it down, almost gagging in the process.

Damn. The stupid things women do for beauty.

I head over to the mirror mounted on the wall near our couch and look at my face. Of course I don't expect it to be immediate, but you never know…

Ugh. I must have had more to drink last night than I realised. My head is spinning.

I lie down on the couch and close my eyes. If I just stay still for a moment…

***

Okay. I think the worst has passed. I am *never* staying up on New Year's Eve again.

I open my eyes and start. What?

How the hell did I end up here?

Somehow, I am lying on the couch in my parents' old living room.

My brain has got to be playing tricks on me. I was literally somewhere else a second ago. This place is almost two hours' drive away!

How much did I drink last night? Did I have a massive blackout? But even if I did, I shouldn't be here. Unless I had a psychotic break and regressed to my teenage years. Shit. I need to get out of here. I don't even know who lives here now.

I stand up and quietly creep towards the door. If I don't wake anyone up, then hopefully I can avoid being arrested.

Just as I'm turning the front door handle, a voice stops me.

"Hey, baby. Happy New Year."

I spin around. What the actual fuck?

It's Maddie. But the old Maddie. I mean, the young Maddie. I can't process this. My legs go from under me, and I collapse to the floor, burying my face in my hands. Maddie hurries over and wraps an arm around my shoulder. "Are you okay? What's wrong?"

"I think I need to see a doctor."

"What? Why? Are you sick?"

"I hope so."

"Eddie, you're scaring me. Should I call an ambulance?"

"I'm not sure." I look up and into her face. "How old are you?"

She laughs. "Really?"

"Yes. Please tell me."

"Does that mean you've forgotten how old you are, too? We're the same age, remember?"

"And that is?" I prod.

She wrinkles her brow. "Eighteen?"

I let out a deep breath. I'm definitely having a breakdown.

"And what date is it?"

"Um, the first of January, 1997?"

Yep. Lost it.

I jump up. "I have to go."

"Where? Nothing's open this morning. I thought we'd just…I don't know…spend a bit of time together in bed…"

"Maybe later," I say distractedly.

She pouts, but I ignore her. I have bigger things to worry about. Like whether my brain is irreparably damaged.

I go outside and look around. It's creepy, seeing everything the way it used to be. The crappy old yard with its sparse lawn and overgrown weeds.

How is this even happening?

I have no idea what to do next, but I know I can't stay here and talk to Maddie when she looks like a goddamn teenager.

I catch my reflection in the window as I pass by.

Okay, that's some next-level shit. I like to think I still look youthful in my forties, but right now I'm an actual freaking kid.

I run down to the river, my lungs heaving, as I try to understand the impossible. I don't think I'm dreaming because I've never had a dream feel this real before. But would it be easier to just pretend I am?

I find a picnic bench down near the water and sit down. I haven't been back here in forever. I didn't exactly have good memories of this town. Especially after…

I curse out loud. Why couldn't I have at least gone back to a couple of months earlier when my mum was still alive? Why did I have to come back just after? If I'm having some sort of breakdown, I could at least get something good out of it.

I hear someone walking behind me, and I half-heartedly turn to see who it is. A guy who looks like a wannabe grunge star walks past. He holds up a wine bottle in my direction. "Happy New Year, bud!"

I ignore him and look back out at the water.

What do I do? Should I check myself into the psych ward at the hospital? I wonder how busy it gets on New Year's Day. I wouldn't be surprised if the emergency department was working overtime.

Maybe if I just do some of that crap mindfulness breathing Anna used to always try to get me to do…

I close my eyes and inhale deeply. In. Out. In. Out.

All right. I'm feeling a little better.

I open my eyes.

I'm still here, looking out at the river. I walk over to a nearby car and stare at myself in the window.

No change.

I walk along Duporth Avenue. What is with this place? Why does the tavern look so weird? And how come that old record store is still there? Didn't it close down ten years ago?

I don't want to go home, well, to whatever this home is. I want to be back in Brisbane. Even Maddie's house in Norman Park would be better than this.

A bus pulls up beside me. I pat the pocket of my shorts and find my wallet. I open it up and see a bunch of bills and coins. That should be enough.

I climb on the bus without even looking where it's headed.

Because it doesn't really matter, does it? This isn't actually happening.

***

I end up in Shell Beach of all places. It's pretty busy, which I guess is to be expected, considering it's New Year's Day. Main Street is teeming with young families and what I assume to be the nineties yuppie crowd.

I have slightly fonder memories of Shell Beach than Maroochydore, because Mum was still alive when we lived here. We had an old single-story brick house in the suburban part of Shell Beach, a five-minute drive from this bus stop.

It was still a shitty town, though. The permanent population was pretty small back in the nineties, so everyone knew everyone else's business. And when your dad was an alcoholic and couldn't hold down a job for longer than a month at a time, people talked.

I remember after Mum died, he tried to get sober, but it didn't last long. I don't know the last time we spoke. I can't even stand to look at him. I'm so glad I didn't follow in his footsteps, although I know I came close. That's why Maddie and I split in the first place.

I head down to the beach and sit on a rock ledge overlooking the sand. Admittedly, the ocean looks pretty inviting—but the nearby restaurants are so dated. Why are they all in shitty shades of yellow and pink? That damn pink!

A couple of teenage girls walk past. I barely pay attention until I hear one of them speak.

"Kelsey! I swear you need to get over Aaron and find someone else. There are so many other guys worth your time…"

"Anna?" I call out.

She stops and looks at me, confused. "Yes?"

"Anna Matthews?"

"Um, no. It's Parnell."

"Oh, shit. Yeah, sorry. I forgot you're not married yet…"

She snorts. "Of course I'm not married yet. I'm seventeen! And where did you get Matthews from?"

The other girl eyes me suspiciously. "Who are you?"

"Uh, I'm Ed. I…" Ugh. What am I supposed to say? *I* don't even know what the hell is going on.

"You're…?" Kelsey prods.

"I…never mind. I think my friend…Ty…must have shown me your photo or something."

"Who's Ty?" she asks, looking even more bewildered than before.

"Never mind. Just ignore me."

Kelsey rolls her eyes at Anna. "Sorry, dude, but you're coming across a little creepy." She grabs Anna's arm and drags her away. Anna looks back over her shoulder as if trying to figure me out, but she doesn't resist Kelsey's pull.

What the fuck is happening?

I head over to a convenience store and buy a Coke. I drink it fast, hoping the sugar and caffeine will kick-start my brain.

When that doesn't work, I figure a walk in the national park might do it.

I head around the point and towards the cove, not really registering the flat turquoise water behind the palm trees. It's weird how few people there are over here. I hate coming here normally, because it's overrun with dickheads training for triathlons. Especially on weekends, which is the only time I would ever get a chance to visit Shell Beach.

I stop when I see a koala in the middle of the path, ambling towards a gum tree. I watch it complete its journey, nestling into a fork and munching on some leaves. The sight relaxes me slightly.

Maybe I've been working too hard, and my brain has rebelled. But then, I've been doing a lot less than usual because of Maddie. Is there such a thing as reverse stress? When you suddenly don't have as much going on and your body decides to stop working properly?

What if I have a brain tumour and this is the way it's manifesting?

Shit? Is this what happened to Mum? What if I inherited something that means I'm about to have an aneurysm, too, and I literally only have a few minutes left to live?

I do think I need to get to the hospital.

I hurry back over to Main Street and find a phone box. I'm just about to call an ambulance when Anna walks past, now alone.

"Hey," I call out.

She narrows her eyes at me. "What?"

"I…uh…I think there might be something wrong with my brain…"

I'm horrified to find that I'm crying. Anna frowns, her eyes full of concern. "Are you in pain?"

"No, but there's a chance I might be about to have an aneurysm."

"Can you even predict that?"

"I have no idea, but something is definitely wrong."

"Do you want me to take you to the hospital?"

"Oh, I was just going to call an ambulance. Could you maybe just wait with me until it arrives?"

"Don't be silly. That will take forever. My car is just over there. Come on."

I gratefully follow her.

"You're not worried I'm an axe murderer?" I ask.

She turns and stares at me. "Well, I wasn't until right now."

"Sorry. I'm not. And I know a real axe murderer would say the same thing, but I'm really not. My name is Ed Matthews and I live in Maroochydore." I get out my licence and show her. "See?"

"It's okay. You're fine. I trust you. I don't know what it is, but you seem kind of familiar. Maybe your friend Ty introduced us one night at a party or something? I still don't know who he is, but sometimes I forget peoples' names."

I can't help smiling. Anna did have a habit of doing that. Even with celebrities, she'd try and tell me a story and forget who she was attempting to describe. "You know, the guy who was in that movie with the girl who was in that TV show? The one with the blonde hair who looks like Kristen Bell?"

"Shell Beach is a small town. I'm sure we have at least a dozen friends in common."

"Probably." She points to a little Mazda 121. "This is mine. Well, my mum's, but she lets me use it. Come on."

I get in the passenger side and put on my seatbelt. "I wonder what Shell Beach Hospital's emergency room will be like today," I muse.

Anna puts on her own seatbelt. "Um, you mean Nambour Hospital?"

"No, I mean…" I stop. Oh. Shell Beach Hospital didn't open until

1999. "Sorry, slip of the tongue. Yeah, I mean Nambour."

"I guess we'll find out soon enough."

"Are you sure you don't mind driving? It's kind of far. And with it being New Year's Day and all…"

"It's fine. Kelsey wanted to go home and sleep, and everyone else is hungover from last night. I was just going to be bored anyway."

"Well, thank you. I appreciate it."

We drive in silence for a while.

"So, before you called me Anna Matthews, but isn't *your* surname Matthews?" she asks.

"Yeah, sorry. Again, it was my brain acting weird. My mum recently died from an aneurysm, and I'm worried I might have inherited the same condition from her."

"I'm so sorry to hear that. But I didn't think that kind of thing was genetic."

"I'm not sure it's a done deal, but there's a small chance it is."

"You poor thing. I'm sure the doctors will be able to check you're okay. And they don't usually mess around with brain stuff, so they'll probably see you quickly."

I study the girl sitting beside me. She definitely got better looking as she aged, but there's something endearing about her as a teenager. The frizzy hair and bushy eyebrows could use a little work, but her face is cute, and those eyes are still the same.

And she didn't think twice about helping a stranger in trouble.

I suddenly feel bad about how terribly I've treated her in the last year. Hell, I've kind of been a shitty partner since we met.

"I hope you have a happy life," I say earnestly.

She giggles. "Um, thanks. I plan on it. After high school, I'm going to save up so I can go to Paris and become a pastry chef. I can't wait."

"You're going to do really well," I say.

"You know this for a fact?" she teases.

"I do," I say firmly.

"All right, then. I appreciate the vote of confidence, even though you have nothing to base it on."

"I just have a feeling."

When we get to the hospital, she pulls up at the emergency entrance. "I'll drop you off here, and then I'll go find a proper parking space. I'll come and meet you in a minute."

"No, no. You go. It could be a while before I see anyone, and I don't want you to waste the first day of the year in the hospital with a stranger."

"I really don't mind."

"I know you don't. But I'll be fine."

"Are you sure?"

"I am. Thanks so much. I don't think many people would take the time to drive a random all the way down here on New Year's Day."

"Like I said, everyone else is hungover."

I open the door and get out, but not before resting a hand on her arm.

"Thanks again. I might see you around one day."

"You might." She gives me a dazzling smile.

I leave and gently close the car door behind me.

At least if I'm about to die, I got to see a familiar face before it happened.

FIVE

Anna

Sunday the 12th January

I've learnt from previous experience that I should do a little prep work before going back in time. Yesterday, I didn't get around to reading the equivalent diary entry for today in 1997 (which I assume is where I'm going), but when I check it now, I'm delighted to see it's a day my parents were away, and Amy was staying at a friend's house. It's like the universe is practically begging me to go back.

I turn off my phone, make sure the apartment is tidy, and have a quick shower. I get back into my PJs and mix up some of the compound.

After drinking it down, I lie on the bed and wait. My body tingles in anticipation of what's about to happen.

The room spins. I close my eyes and wait for the feeling to stop.

After a few moments, I sense a change in the atmosphere. I think I'm there.

The sun is shining through the cracks in the blinds in my old bedroom. It's just after 7am, and the house is silent.

After a quick check in my diary to confirm that I am, in fact, back in 1997 (I am), I jump up and head down the hall. Amy's room is empty as expected.

"Hello?"

No answer.

I go through the house to double-check that Mum and Dad aren't around either.

They're not. Perfect.

Today is going to be amazing.

I enjoy a leisurely breakfast while I lie by the pool. January in Shell Beach has always been preferable to Brisbane, thanks to its proximity to the ocean. Plus, I can legally drive now. There's nothing holding me back.

Just after 9am, I phone Kurt's house. I have a couple of scenarios planned in my head for why I'm calling. I figure I'll see what time he's working and go from there.

"Hello?" A female voice answers.

"Uh, hi. Is Kurt there?"

"Who wants to know?"

"Please tell him it's Anna."

"Why should I do that, Anna? Are you fucking him?"

Okaaay…so I'm probably not talking to his sister. Unless she's super possessive. And psychotic.

"No. But is it any of your business?"

"Yes, it's my goddamn business! I'm the only one who fucks Kurt, so fuck off!"

She slams down the phone, and I stare at it incredulously.

That was unexpected. Not to mention depressing.

Kurt has a girlfriend now? I suppose he has one in the future. Why shouldn't he also have one in 1997?

All my grand plans go swirling down the drain.

So much for the universe wanting me to be here. Maybe it wanted to tell me once and for all to give up and move on.

I trudge upstairs to the shower to drown my sorrows. My Flex shampoo and strawberry body wash make me want to cry.

I feel so alone.

But then I decide it would be a shame to just lie around the house in 1997, when I could still be doing other stuff that I'm unable to do in the future.

And I know just where to start.

***

"Anna! What a lovely surprise! What brings you here today?"

"I just wanted to see you, Grandma."

She beams, and I'm glad I made the decision to come here. It only just occurs to me that I should have used the compound more before now purely to see her.

"That's lovely, dear."

"How do you feel about getting out of here for a few hours?"

"And do what?"

"Anything you like."

"Really?"

"Yes! Why not?"

"I'm sure you have better things to do on a Sunday than waste time with your grandmother."

"Believe me, there is nothing I want to do more."

"Are you sure?"

"I am. Now stop being difficult and come on!"

She laughs. "All right, then. Let me just get my purse."

I take Grandma's arm, and she shuffles beside me out to the car. I help her into the passenger side and jump into the driver's seat.

"What would you like to do first?" I have visions of taking her around town like Macklemore did with his grandma and egging people's houses— but somehow, I don't think mine would be into that kind of thing.

"I'd kill for a decent cup of coffee. The stuff they offer at the village tastes like dirt."

I laugh. "Easy." I start driving down the road before realising I have no idea where you can get good coffee in Maroochydore in 1997.

"How about we go to The Palace?" I suggest. "They're bound to have at least one place that sells good coffee."

"Whatever you think is best."

"Is there anything else you want to do while we're there?"

"I don't think so, honey. But if we have time, I would like to go down to the river and sit in the shade for a while."

"That sounds perfect."

We park at The Palace and find a Coffee Club. It's not as fancy as the ones in the future, but it's good enough. I order Grandma a cappuccino, and a hot chocolate for me. Despite my best efforts, I still find myself regressing in small ways whenever I'm back here. It still feels weird to order a double-shot espresso for my teenage self.

We sit down in the corner, and Grandma looks around as if she's taking in every single detail.

"This is nice," she says wistfully. "I forget what it's like in the real world sometimes."

"Doesn't Mum ever take you out?"

"Oh, she does, but it always feels so rushed. Like she's on a mission or something. We very rarely just sit at a coffee shop and talk."

"I'm sorry. And I apologise for not doing this more myself."

"Don't be silly. I know you're busy with work and school…and boys." Her eyes twinkle at the last part.

"Not too busy for you, though."

"Oh, I know I'm just a foolish old woman. You're probably already regretting this outing."

53

I gape. "Grandma! You are not foolish, and I am not regretting this! How could you say something like that?" I know I already told her my career plans the last time I saw her, but this is a different timeline and I want her to know again. "You have no idea how influential you've been on my life! Because of you, I'm going to enrol in a cooking school in France after I graduate, and I'm going to be a pastry chef. You've inspired me so much!"

Her face softens and she holds out her arms. I lean in to accept her hug.

"I'm honoured that you hold me in such high regard."

A waiter brings over our drinks, and we sit in companionable silence, slowly sipping from our mugs. Every now and again I glance at Grandma and smile. I can't believe that through some weird rip in the fabric of time, I'm allowed to spend time with her again.

I let her set the pace and wait until she's ready to leave before we wander out across the road to the river. I find us a picnic bench, and we sit down, facing the water. We're not far from where Kurt and I had a drink together that one time.

"Oh! I just thought of something I want!" Grandma says suddenly.

"What's that?"

"I've been showing one of the gentlemen at the village my music collection, and I realised I can't find my old Andrews Sisters record. I was hoping to perhaps buy another copy so we could listen to it together."

"Is this gentleman called Noel, by any chance?"

Her eyes widen. "How do you know Noel? Has he said something?"

"I've just seen how you two look at each other. He seems like a nice man." I hope she doesn't call my bluff, because I really have no idea what he looks like.

"Well, don't tell your mother. I'm not ashamed of our relationship, but

I'm afraid she might not understand. She was always such a daddy's girl. I don't think she'd cope knowing there's someone else in my life."

"You might be surprised. But don't worry. Your secret's safe with me."

She smiles, relieved. "I'll tell her when the time is right."

"Anyway, back to your question about the record. Yes, I think I know somewhere that might sell what you're looking for."

And even a particular staff member who might serve us. I'm tempted to look up another music store in the area, because I almost can't bear to run into Kurt knowing he has a girlfriend—but at the same time, I can't help myself. I'd already been contemplating dropping by his work later, just to catch a glimpse of him, and now I have a legitimate reason.

"Is it nearby? I can't walk far."

"As a matter of fact, it's only about two minutes from here."

"Excellent."

We get up and make our way back to the road. My heart beats faster and faster the closer we get to the store. By the time we actually reach the door, I'm ready to pass out.

"Are you okay, sweetie? You look a little pale," Grandma says.

"I'm...I'm fine."

"*I* should be the one out of breath from walking that short distance, not you," she teases.

"I'm all right. Probably just a little run down," I improvise.

I brace myself and push open the door, letting Grandma walk ahead of me into the musty interior.

It only takes me a second to see that Kurt's not here. My stomach drops, which is ridiculous, considering I knew nothing was going to happen anyway. But I so badly wanted to see him. Grandma shuffles on ahead and starts flicking through the albums in the Golden Oldies section. The guy at the counter looks up briefly but seems to write us off as timewasters and doesn't even say hello. I wonder if Kurt still works here. Rachel mentioned he was only employed for a year, so maybe he already left. When I first met him, he told me he worked every weekend, so it's not a good sign if he's not in today.

I glance at the doorway at the back of the shop where we first hung out, listening to Bob Dylan. I think I knew even then he'd be trouble. And then I wonder if I made Ed leave me because of my feelings towards Kurt. Could I have been that stupid and selfish? Why would I ruin my marriage because of some temporary liaison with a guy who doesn't even know who I am?

No. It can't be true. I did love Ed, but he loved Maddie—and I know I tried to make our marriage work. It just wasn't meant to be.

I feel a tear roll down my cheek. Jeez. I have to get it together.

The front door opens, letting a warm breeze in. I turn reflexively to see who it is.

My eyes widen.

It's Kurt.

He heads behind the counter and starts rummaging around in a cupboard.

"The pays ready yet, buddy?" he asks the other guy.

"Oh, yeah. Just in the drawer."

I watch as he bends down and pops back up, holding an envelope. "Rad. I have a ton of bills to sort out this week, but I'm also hoping to get tickets to see Faith No More. They go on sale next week."

"Oh right, yeah. Me, too. You already going with anyone?"

"Nope. You want to catch a ride with me?"

"Sounds good. I know someone who might be able to get us decent seats. I'll keep you posted."

"Thanks, dude."

He then seems to notice me. I quickly wipe my cheek and pray my eyes aren't bloodshot. I quickly glance over at Grandma, but she's distracted by the albums in front of her.

Kurt shoots me a look, one of those knowing, cheeky looks—as if he's keeping a secret he doesn't want to share. I blush involuntarily.

He sidles over and looks down at the albums I've started frantically flicking through. "Hey."

"Uh, hey."

"Has Mark already served you? Or is he being his usual antisocial self?"

"Excuse me!" Mark protests. "I can hear you, you know."

"I do know. I was making a point." He holds a hand beside his mouth conspiratorially. "He's a bit of a tortured artist, that Mark."

"Ah."

"So, did you need any help?"

"Oh, no, thanks. I was just looking at…" I pick an album at random. "This."

He raises an eyebrow. "You're a Slayer fan?"

"Yes," I say indignantly.

He roars with laughter. "I like you. What are you doing right now?"

"Besides talking to you?"

"Yes. Besides talking to me."

"I'm actually here with my grandma." I point to her in the corner. "She's looking for something by the Andrews Sisters."

He looks over at her curiously. "You know, I think I might be able to help her. Hang on."

He heads over to the Golden Oldies section and stands beside Grandma. I almost melt at the sight of them together.

"You're an Andrews Sisters fan, huh?"

"I am," she confirms. "Can you help me?"

"I can, indeed." Within seconds, he locates a Best Of album and hands it to her. "Will this do?"

She takes it from him, beaming. "This will do just fine."

"If you promise not to tell anyone, I'll give you a discount," he whispers.

"Oh, I wouldn't want to get you in trouble," she says, waving a hand dismissively.

"It's all good." He winks at me. "And were you going to take that Slayer album?"

"Actually, I might leave it today," I say, smiling. I turn to Grandma. "Now you'll be able to show Noel your music."

She gives me a warning look, and Kurt notices. "Oh? Who's this Noel? He must be special."

"He's a man at the village where my grandma lives," I answer for her.

"In that case…"

He turns back to the Golden Oldies and pulls out another record. "Take this one, too. No charge."

Grandma looks at the cover and her face lights up. "Benny Goodman! But I couldn't possibly…"

"No arguing. The manager is trying to clear out some of our older stock, so you'd be doing us a favour."

"Are you sure?"

"Yes. That will be ten dollars for the Andrews Sisters album."

I want to throw myself at this man and make out with him right now.

"As long as you're sure."

"I'm sure." He takes the ten-dollar bill my grandma hands him and puts the two records in a paper bag before giving them back to her.

"Thank you, young man. You've been very helpful. Now, why don't I help you? What do you think of my granddaughter here?"

My mouth falls open. "Grandma!"

She ignores me and looks expectantly at Kurt. He appears to be stifling a laugh.

"You can't ask that!" I say, giving him an out. "His girlfriend would get mad if she knew what you were trying to do."

Kurt chuckles. "Actually, she wouldn't. Because I don't have one."

My heart catches in my throat. He doesn't? Then who was that girl on the phone earlier?

"Great. Then let me formally introduce you to Anna. Will you take her off my hands for a few hours?" My grandmother is enjoying herself immensely. I, on the other hand, am mortified.

"I will gladly take her off your hands, but only if she wants to."

I look from Grandma to Kurt and back again.

"Is this your way of getting rid of me so you can go and listen to records with Noel?"

"Yes."

I roll my eyes. "Well, at least you're honest." I look at Kurt, embarrassed. "I'll just take Grandma home and then I'll come back. But if you have other stuff to do, I totally understand."

He grins. "You're not getting away that easily. I'll be here."

"All right. I won't be long."

Grandma and I leave the store and walk back to the car.

"I can't believe you just did that!" I say, once we have our seatbelts on.

"He seemed like a lovely man, and I could tell you liked him."

"How could you tell that?" I demand.

"I just know these things. And he liked you, too. Why else would he give me two albums for ten dollars?"

I smile. "Because he could see you were a cool grandma. Anyway, thank you."

59

"You're welcome."

We get back to the home, and I lead my grandmother inside. "I had a lovely morning," I say, giving her a kiss on the cheek.

"I did as well," she says. "I haven't had that much fun in ages."

"You mean you haven't had a chance to meddle in ages."

"Ha. Off you go. It's almost lunchtime. Noel will be wondering where I am."

"Have fun. I'll talk to you again soon."

"I expect you to tell me all about your date when I next see you."

"It's not a date. But okay. And I want to hear about yours, too! I love you, Grandma."

"I love you, too, sweetie."

I watch as she heads towards the central dining room, and I shake my head.

Who would have thought that my grandmother would play an integral part in reuniting me with Kurt?

The true test will be if he's still there when I get back.

I can't wait to find out.

SIX

I hurry back to the record store and see that Kurt is, in fact, there, standing out the front. I can't believe my luck—but I need to find out who I was talking to earlier before we go any further.

"You waited!" I say happily.

"You came back!" He matches my enthusiasm.

"Well, I had to thank you again for being so generous with my grandma."

"She's really sweet. It's obvious she cares about you. And it's great that you get to spend time with her. I wish my grandparents were still alive so I could hang out with them."

"My grandma is awesome. I really enjoy her company. I think if we all paid more attention to our grandparents, the world would be a better and wiser place."

"I agree." He looks at me with such intensity, I shiver.

"So, you really don't have a girlfriend waiting for you at home or anything?"

"Nope. No girlfriend. Although, I do have a psycho ex who showed up at my house this morning. That's why I'm here. I asked her to leave, and she wouldn't, so I did instead."

"Oh! Right." So that was the woman on the phone. The psycho ex.

"I'm Kurt, by the way."

"I know."

He wrinkles his brow. "You do?"

"I've seen you in the store before. You wear a name badge."

He laughs. "Of course I do."

"I think I've seen you in there on a Sunday before…"

"Oh, yeah. I normally work weekends, but Mark wanted to swap a shift with me. I was actually looking forward to a Sunday to myself until Charli showed up. But thanks to your grandma, the day has been redeemed, and I get to spend the afternoon with you."

"And my grandma got me out of her hair so she could go and flirt with a man called Noel," I joke, so I don't do something stupid like rub myself all over him.

His face turns serious for a second. "Please don't be freaked out by what I'm about to say, but you seem really familiar. And not just because you might have visited the shop once or twice. I feel like we should have known each other before now."

A tiny thrill zooms through my body. He stills feels the same!

"Maybe we met in a previous life," I say mysteriously.

"Maybe. Do you believe in reincarnation?"

"I'm not sure. But I've recently started believing in parallel universes."

"So, you think we might have already met in one of those?"

"Definitely. If every possible combination of everything that has ever happened is out there somewhere, then we would have met for sure."

Several times, in fact.

"How old are you? You seem very mature for someone so young."

"Age is just a number, I've decided."

He laughs. "I agree. So, are you sure this is all okay, spending time with me?"

Is he kidding?

"It's more than okay," I assure him.

"Excellent. What would you like to do?"

"How about I surprise you?"

"I'd love that."

I lead him back to my car and we both climb in. "You don't have to be anywhere by a particular time?" I ask.

"Nope. I'm free as a bird. In fact, the longer I stay out, the better. I'm hoping Charli will be gone by the time I get back."

"What's her deal?"

"She dropped by unannounced this morning and wouldn't leave. She doesn't even like me anymore, but she can't handle the idea of me being happy and moving on."

I drive in the direction of Shell Beach. "How long were you two together?"

"Only a couple of months around October last year. Then she went on some Contiki tour to Bali with a bunch of her girlfriends and apparently fell in love with a Balinese masseuse. She stayed over there for a while until he cheated on her, and then she came crawling back to me. I was over her by then, but now she won't leave me alone. It's driving me crazy."

"You poor thing."

"I'm sure she'll get bored soon. I just have to be firm."

I turn on the radio and tune it to one of the alternative stations. Bush's *Glycerine* is playing.

"Don't feel like you have to listen to this music for my benefit," he says.

"I like it!" I protest. "I mean, I was kind of stretching it with the Slayer stuff, but I pretty much like anything."

"Good to know."

"Pop is great, but so is alternative."

"Do you want to know a secret?" he asks, giving me a conspiratorial smile.

"What?"

"I own a Shaggy album."

I try not to laugh. "You like *Shaggy*?"

"I do."

"That's awesome. I would never have guessed that someone who looks like Eddie Vedder would admit to liking anything but grunge."

"You think I resemble Eddie Vedder?" He seems very pleased by this.

I want to say I think he's even cuter than Eddie, but that might be overdoing it.

"You do, and you know it," I tease.

He sits there, a big smile on his face.

I think about how he's a dance music producer in the future and wonder when he became interested in that genre.

"Do you listen to any dance music?" I ask.

"A bit. You?"

I know I listened to a little back then, but I can't remember exactly what. I notice a CD wallet on the floor.

"Have a look at my collection," I say, pointing to it.

He picks it up, grinning. "You're not worried I'm going to judge you for your secret love of *The Macarena*?"

"I hate *The Macarena*!"

"I'm sure there must be one embarrassing album in here..." He flicks through the sleeves. I have to keep my eyes on the road, but I'm equally curious to see what's in there.

After a minute, he pulls one out. "Larkin?"

"Oh, yeah! You know them?"

"No. Any good?"

"They're great! Kelsey and I saw them on a late-night music show, and we were hooked. Put on *Darkness*."

I'd totally forgot about that track. I used to be obsessed with it.

Kurt slots the CD into the player and skips to track four.

He leans back and closes his eyes.

I glance at his expression, and if I'm not mistaken, I'd say he looks euphoric.

When the track ends, he doesn't say anything.

"What did you think?" I ask when I can't take the suspense any longer.

"Amazing. I can't believe I haven't heard them until now."

"Their other songs are pretty good, too."

Kurt insists on listening to the whole album all the way up the coast road.

When we arrive at the national park, he finally realises where we are.

"Wow. How did we get here so quickly?"

"I guess good music can have that effect on you," I say, smiling.

"True." He gets out of the car. "This is exactly what I felt like doing."

"I'm glad. Are you happy to walk around the bay?"

"Yes!"

We walk side by side along the sandy path, underneath the gum trees.

"Tell me a little about you, Anna. Do you have any brothers or sisters?"

"I have a sister called Amy. She's a few years younger than me."

"I have a half-brother. He's only eight."

"Oh, wow. That's a big age gap."

"Yeah. My mum and dad split up when I was ten and Dad remarried. He had Bodhi with his new wife."

"Are you close with everyone?"

"Sort of. Mum and Dad don't talk anymore, so it can make the holidays a bit stressful. I'm probably closer with my cousins. They live here in Shell

Beach, actually."

"What are their names?" I ask, knowing full well what his reply will be.

"Chris and Rachel Morgan."

"I know them!" I say, feigning happy surprise. "I go to school with Rachel. She's a good friend of mine!"

"That's crazy! And awesome."

"I know."

"I'm not really allowed at their house, though, because their dad doesn't like me."

Ah, yes. Because of the Metallica concert where Chris got his nose pierced by a random stranger, and Kurt was supposed to be the responsible guardian.

"That's a shame."

"We figure it out. And Chris is eighteen now, so he can pretty much do what he wants. Rachel won't be far behind."

We pick our way through the pandanus palms and over the rocks down to a secluded beach. The ocean is glittery, and the air temperature is perfect. I look back at the hill behind us and note that there aren't any other people walking along the trail.

"You are so lucky to live this close to the park," Kurt says, spreading his arms out and turning in a circle.

"I need to come here more often," I agree.

We sit down on the sand, and Kurt rolls over onto one side, facing me.

"What?" I ask, suddenly feeling shy.

"I'm glad your grandma set us up."

"I'm glad, too."

The sun beats down on us. I hope I don't get sunburned.

"I wish I brought sunscreen," I tell him.

"Oh, I have some. Hang on." He rummages around in the small

backpack he brought with him and hands me a bottle of 15+.

I'm impressed. "Were you a Boy Scout back in the day or something?"

"No, I just know I'll probably end up at the beach most days, and I don't want to get skin cancer."

"You're not just a pretty face, huh?"

"That's right."

I rub some of the cream over my arms, legs, and face. And then I look at him. It's too good an opportunity to pass up.

"Do you want me to do you?"

He laughs. "Isn't that normally what the guy says?"

"I don't know. Is it?"

He lifts off his T-shirt. "Go on, then."

My eyes go immediately to the tanned skin of his chest. He has a tattoo of what looks like a bunch of stars placed in a random formation.

"I like your tattoo," I say, tracing one of the stars with my finger.

"Oh, yeah, it's supposed to be the Jewel Box. It's..."

"...next to the left point of the southern cross," I finish for him.

He looks at me in shock. "How did you know that?"

"Someone told me once," I say. "When did you get the tattoo?"

"Last year. Around June, I think."

I stare at him. "Could it have been around the twenty-fifth?"

He raises an eyebrow. "Maybe. Why?"

"What made you choose that date?"

"I don't know." He thinks for a second. "I'm pretty sure I'd been up here the day before and gone to the beach that night with a couple of friends, and the stars were really bright. I'd always planned to get the tattoo at some point, but it finally felt like the right timing. Why?"

Because in an alternate reality, I spent that night with you, and you said the Jewel Box would remind you of me from that point.

"Oh, no reason. I almost got a tattoo on that day, but I chickened out at the last minute."

Nice save.

"Ha. Wouldn't it have been weird if we were at the studio together, only separated by a wall?"

"It would."

"Wouldn't your parents have had to give you permission to get the tattoo?"

"Oh, yeah, they trust me to make my own decisions," I improvise. "But I think they were secretly happy when I decided not to go ahead."

"There'll be plenty of time to reconsider later."

I keep staring at the stars on his chest. "I really like yours."

"Are you into astronomy?"

"Not as much as I'd like."

"I'll teach you a bit sometime."

I pour some of the sunscreen into my hand and gently massage it into his chest. He raises an eyebrow, smiling, but doesn't say anything.

I take my time, working my way down to his bellybutton and over his arms and neck.

"I'll let you do your face," I say.

"Can I do this first?" He gently pushes me down onto my back before pressing his mouth to mine.

I close my eyes, dizzy from the sensory overload. It's been so long since I've been with this man, I was afraid it would never happen again. And this is the first time I can really relax into the moment and enjoy every guilt-free second of kissing my grunge god.

He peppers my neck with tiny feathery kisses. "Thank you for taking a chance on me today. I'm so glad I decided to go into the record store on my day off."

"Me, too," I say, wrapping my arms around him and pulling him even closer. "Me, too."

***

We kiss for what feels like forever. I wouldn't mind if we stayed this way until my time was up, but then I think of something. I sit up suddenly.

"Hey, what's your…" An electronic beeping sound interrupts us.

"Sorry," Kurt says. "That's my phone. I only just got it, and not many people have the number yet, but the ones that do are important." He opens his backpack and pulls out a handset that looks like a walkie talkie.

"Yeah?"

He furrows his brow as he listens to the person on the other end.

"Seriously?"

He glances at me and frowns. Uh-oh.

"Okay. I'm just at Shell Beach, but I'll leave now."

He hangs up and sighs. "I have to go. That was my roommate, Jay. He just got home and said the house has been trashed, and a pile of my stuff is on fire in the front yard."

"Oh my God! Charli?"

"I assume so. I don't know anyone else who would be that upset with me. I better go and sort it out. I'm so sorry."

"Don't be silly. You definitely need to go. I'll drive you."

"No, no. I'll catch the bus. I don't expect you to take me all the way down and then come back up."

"I don't mind, honestly."

"It's better if I go alone. I don't want to expose you to Charli if she's still hanging around."

"As long as you're sure."

"I am." He pulls me up, so my legs are wrapped around his waist, and kisses me again. "I don't want to leave."

"We'll see each other soon," I say, trying hard to hide my disappointment. If only he knew I'll have to start all over again after today.

"You bet we will. Can I call you later?"

"Of course you can."

I type my number into his phone, and he types his into mine.

"I'm important enough to have your mobile number?" I tease.

"Apparently you are."

We walk in silence back to the car before I drop him at the bus stop.

He pulls me in one last time for a hug. I breathe in his warmth, wishing I could manipulate time more.

"Bye, Anna."

"Bye, Kurt."

I watch him walk off, feeling both happy and sad.

And then I remember I didn't get to finish asking my question.

What's your surname?

SEVEN

I head home for the rest of the day. I don't know what time Mum, Dad and Amy are due back, but I don't mind either way.

I keep my phone nearby, just in case Kurt decides he wants to see me again before I leave and wander aimlessly around the house.

I feel like I shouldn't be wasting the precious time I have here, but I don't know what else to do.

I have a swim, make myself a snack, and get sucked into watching an episode of *Spin City*. Oh, it's Michael J Fox! I feel like I have an affinity with him via *Back to the Future* since becoming a time traveller. At least my version doesn't let me mess up the future. It's frustrating, but it also takes a lot of the pressure off.

My phone rings around 6pm.

"Hello?"

"Hi, Anna? It's Kurt."

"I know," I smile.

"How are you? Sorry again about leaving you earlier."

"Um, your stuff was literally on fire. I think I can forgive you. What happened with Charli?"

"Oh, she was gone before I got back, and my roommate had hosed down my stuff as best he could, so there wasn't much for me to do. I did call the police, though, and I'm in the process of organising a restraining order."

"I'm so sorry you have to deal with that. Were you able to rescue any of your things?"

"Not really. But there was nothing that valuable in there. Thankfully, most of my albums were in Jay's room, and he was still asleep with his door locked when she decided to trash the place. So, I really only lost a few clothes and books."

"That's a relief."

"I'm more annoyed that I didn't get to spend more time with you."

"It's okay."

"What are you doing tomorrow?"

Probably working on my new business more than twenty years in the future.

"Not much."

"Can I take you out to dinner tomorrow night?"

"Sure." I know it's not possible, but I can still act like it is.

"Great. Thanks again for such an amazing morning. I'll talk to you soon."

"Bye."

I hang up and head to my room. It would have been nice to see Kurt for a little while longer today, but I'm definitely not complaining about the time we got to spend together at the national park. I'll have a pretty amazing memory to sustain me in the present.

At least for a day or so.

***

I drift through the next few days in a bit of a daze. I really want to use the compound again, but with less than two weeks until Naughty or Nice opens, I need to concentrate on making this business venture a success. It won't work if I'm sleeping entire days away.

On Thursday, Kelsey and I meet up with Amy at the café to check on its progress.

"Oh my God. Amy, this is amazing!"

My sister beams. "I know."

Kelsey thought it would be a good idea to exploit my already well-known brand, so the *naughty* part of the business name represents my signature French pastries, and the *nice* is the best recipes from my healthy dessert blog. I had the idea to furnish it half in pink and half in black.

I pretend to be a customer and walk slowly towards the counter, taking in all the details. Now seeing the finished result, I know I made the right call. The floor is lined with black and white tiles, and the walls are painted a baby pink. The stools look like cupcakes, and there are two counters— one black and one pink—with a small gap for staff to walk between.

But the focal point is definitely the chandelier, and it gives the whole café a luxe vibe. The overall effect is even better than I hoped.

Kelsey emits a low whistle. "You've outdone yourself, Amy."

"Thanks. It was fun. I don't normally get to do something so bright and unique. Everybody wants white and beige these days."

"Well, you and your colleagues are welcome to come in and eat whatever you like anytime, free of charge," I tell her.

"You'll be sorry you offered. The guys I work with have big appetites, and they're huge fans of your cooking."

During the design process, I often sent batches of test recipes to Amy's staff for feedback. It made me feel less guilty about not paying for Amy's labour.

"It's the least I can do."

Amy looks at her phone. "I have to get back to the office but let me know if you need anything else before you open."

"Will do." I wrap her up in a huge hug and she laughs. "Stop! You know I don't do hugs."

I squeeze her harder.

She squeaks in protest and then extricates herself. "All right. Talk later!"

Kelsey and I continue our inspection of the premises.

"This will be the coolest place I've ever worked," Kelsey says. "And the fact that it's ours makes it even better!"

We both ended up using quite a bit of our savings to fund the venture. I figured I didn't need to buy another house right away, and Kelsey had always thought owning property was overrated. "I like to be able to move whenever I want," she pointed out when we talked about it a while back. "For example, I couldn't have relocated to Brisbane so quickly if I owned somewhere at Shell Beach."

I run a hand along the smooth black counter. "Are you ready for opening day?"

"Yes! I wish it was tomorrow! But I know we still have a lot of work to do. How are you going with kitchen staff?"

"All good. I have two definites—Coco and Owen—and then Harriet as a possible extra if we need her later. Have you sent out offers to the wait staff?"

"I have. I went with Jax, Emery and Xander."

"Great. And they all accepted?"

"Yep. I think they're in awe of you. I never knew you were so famous!"

I laugh. "Um, I'm not, but thank you."

"You have no idea, do you? I've contacted some of the local media, and they're all really excited to promote you."

"Aw, I'm glad." I really did not know I was that big of a deal. Sure, I was aware of my online following, and I get enough royalties from my published cookbook to see it does well, but it never occurred to me that the average person on the street knew who I was.

I go over to our fancy new coffee machine and switch it on. While I wait for it to heat up, I prepare some coffee beans in the grinder and get out the milk. My eyes glaze over as I remember my time with Kurt the other day.

"Are you still thinking about last weekend?" Kelsey asks.

I jump. "What do you mean?"

"I mean the fight you had with Rachel. Why? What did you think I meant?"

"Oh, nothing. Actually, to be honest, I've been too busy to think about her, but I'm still disappointed she stayed with Billy instead of coming home with me."

"I talked to her yesterday."

"You did?"

"Yeah, she told me the full story. Apparently, she believed you when you said the kiss wasn't welcome, but she was bummed out by the whole situation. Plus, she had another guy to worry about who was still inside."

"Well, she could have tried a bit harder to contact me afterwards! She didn't exactly act like she believed me."

"Didn't she call *and* text you? I think maybe she was upset that you didn't want to see her the next day and sort everything out then."

"Whatever. I can't be bothered with that crap now." I feel like she should have known to call me again once I'd calmed down a little.

"She *does* want to talk to you and clear the air. If you just phone her…"

"She can phone me if she wants to talk."

Kelsey shakes her head. "All right. I'm not going to hassle either of you anymore. I just hope you don't let your friendship go because of a silly misunderstanding."

"It's not silly." Of course Kelsey wouldn't see it as big a deal as me, because she was in the same situation as Rachel back when we had our falling out. She probably thinks if she sides with me, it's like admitting she was wrong all along.

I busy myself by wiping down the bench and heating the milk. My thoughts drift back to what I thought Kelsey was talking about when she mentioned the weekend. I can still feel Kurt's lips on mine…that smooth chest pressed against my body…

Eventually, Kelsey notices. Probably because I haven't been paying attention to the milk and it's now frothing all over the counter.

"Babe, what's going on?"

"Sorry, I was just thinking."

"About what?"

"How things might have been different depending on the decisions I made when I was younger."

"Where's this coming from?"

"I don't know."

"Are you unhappy with where you are right now?"

"No. Not at all. I mean, I love that you and I are about to start this project together. I was thinking more about Ed…"

And specifically, if I had done things differently in the original 1996, or even 1997, would I have met Kurt and ended up with him instead?

But I can't tell Kelsey that. Or can I? It's been killing me not to have anyone to talk to about the compound. The younger version of Kelsey seemed to think I could prove to her that it was real by telling her I knew about her high school crush on Mr. Green.

"No one knows what any of their decisions will mean in the long term. Hell, I could have chosen to cut school that time Prince Harry visited Shell Beach, and he would have married me instead of Meghan."

I laugh. And then I think about how I ran into Kurt on Shell Beach on a day I cut school the second time around. Which illustrates my point.

"You know one thing I do regret?" she muses.

"What?"

"Giving Aaron so much of my attention back in high school. He *so* wasn't worth it."

Screw it. I'm going to tell her.

I clear my throat. "Um, if I tell you something, will you promise to give me the benefit of the doubt before you accuse me of lying or being mentally unstable?"

She narrows her eyes. "I don't know. Do you think I will end up reacting that way?"

"Possibly, but I need to share this with someone."

"You're kind of scaring me, babe, but go on."

I put the milk down and wipe my hands on my pants. "All right. Well, you know how Ed and Maddie are together now?"

"Uh, duh."

"Well, I never explained fully what happened there."

"What *did* happen there?"

I take a deep breath and go to my handbag to retrieve the youth compound. I keep it with me at all times now since Maddie accidentally took it from my bathroom. I hand Kelsey the jar. She reads the label. "Okaaayyy…I'm assuming this is that compound you were so desperate to find the other day. How has that got anything to do with what you want to confess?"

"This isn't just an anti-aging formula. It actually puts you back in your teenage body."

Kelsey frowns. "What the hell, Anna? You seriously think I'm that gullible?"

"I know, I know," I say quickly. "It sounds totally nuts, and I completely understand if you don't believe me—but for me, it's the truth.

I have been back to the nineties after taking this stuff."

"Let me try it, then," she says. I'm guessing she's thinking that will bring an abrupt end to my practical joke.

"Oh, okay. But I need to prepare you first. The effects last twelve hours, so you might not want to take a dose right this second. Unless you're happy to stay here at the café until the morning?"

"Really? And what? I'll just be lying comatose on the floor?"

"I guess. I've never had anyone around to see what happens to me when I take it. I always timed it so I was on my own. But I assume it just looks like I'm sleeping."

Her expression changes to one of a person humouring someone they very clearly believe to be experiencing psychotic delusions. To be honest, I don't blame her, but I'm more than happy for her to try it out. I want to see if it works the same way on her.

She opens the jar and sniffs its contents. "Seriously, though. What is this stuff?"

"I have no idea, but it hasn't caused me any permanent damage that I know of."

"That you know of." She shakes her head. "Where did you get it?"

"My sponsor sent it over." I leave out the fact that they don't seem to have ever heard of it. "I was telling the truth when I told you that."

"Why don't you take it?" she asks me.

"I can if you want. You can let me know what happens to my body here while I'm there. I've been wondering if I can be woken up during the twelve hours it's in effect."

"Hang on, hang on. I need you to start at the beginning. Tell me everything from the first time you tried it up until now. And then I'll make a decision on your sanity."

"Okay." I start with how I woke up in her bedroom on that first day, which was the day of Rachel's party and when I broke up with Todd. I go through everything I can remember, but I leave out any mention of Kurt for now. That would just complicate matters. I tell her about how I tracked down Ed and met Maddie, and how I got to see Grandma Millie again. But I also tell her how nothing in the future changes as a result of anything new that happens in the past—and that each visit stands alone, too.

She shakes her head. "This is insane."

"I know. But there was one thing you told me to say in the future as a way of proving I was telling the truth."

She raises an eyebrow. "And what was that?"

"That you were obsessed with Mr. Green."

She bursts out laughing and covers her mouth. "Oh my God! I totally was! But I'm sure I told you that in this reality."

"You didn't. I swear."

"I can't be sure either way, so I'm afraid I'll need further proof."

"Well, there are two ways to find out. Either you take it, or I do."

"Or we take it together?"

"I guess. I wonder if we'd end up in the same reality?"

"All right. How about I take it, then? And you can monitor me?"

"If you're sure."

She thinks for a second. "As long as I don't die from ingesting this stuff."

"I don't think you will. I haven't, obviously."

"Gee, your certainty is overwhelming."

"Well, do you want me to take it? I can find out anything you've been wondering about from the past. Ooh, ooh! Wait! We should go back to my place first. I have all my old diaries there, so I can check in advance what happened that day."

Kelsey shakes her head. "I can't believe I'm going along with this."

"If I wake up tomorrow and can't answer any questions about the mission you set me, then you can decide what to make of it all."

"Fine. Let's get this over with."

I clap my hands together. I'm so glad Kelsey hasn't completely written me off.

We drive back to my place, and I race over to the bookshelf to get my diary. I shove it in her face. "Here. This is what happened the first time. If it triggers anything, I can then go and find out about it."

She gingerly takes the diary from me and opens it. "How does this work?"

"I've been going back to the same day, just in 1997. Well, 1996 until recently."

She flicks to today's date and starts to laugh.

"Man, we were such dorks." She points to a line. "You wrote a fan letter to Brian Austin Green?"

"Ha. I know. I was so obsessed with *90210*. It's funny, because you don't think you change much over time, but you really do. Although, I don't think you change where it matters. I hung out with you a few times in 1996 this time around, and you are almost the same."

"Aw, babe. I appreciate the sentiment, even if it's coming from a deluded place." She continues skimming the entry. "It says here we went down to The Palace because I wanted to find Aaron, but we didn't end up seeing him. Oh! I just thought of something! I had this old tin that I put a bunch of mementos in, and I buried it somewhere. Ask the earlier version of me where it is and tell me what's inside. Then I'll believe you."

I roll my eyes. "And this thing is still buried now?"

"Yep."

"Okay. I'll do my best."

"I suppose you better get moving, then."

"Jeez, you're bossy."

"I just want to get this charade over with. And then I can proceed to tease you mercilessly about the time you tried to prank me and failed."

"You'll see I'm telling the truth."

"Whatever. Anyway, I'll try and wake you up after an hour, but if I can't, I won't panic until the twelve hours are up."

"Sounds like a plan. Oh, but I usually sleep all night, too, so I'm not sure what happens there." I look at the clock. "It's almost 3pm now, so maybe you're best off just coming back in the morning if you can't wake me up. Or you can crash here?"

"I can't believe I'm actually going along with this, but okay. I'll stay overnight—although I might go home and get a change of clothes at some point. You don't have anything you need to take care of before you go?"

"Nope. I'll eat when I wake up in 1997."

She snorts. "Sure you will."

I go to the kitchen to get a glass of water and a spoon. I mix the compound in front of Kelsey and then head to the bedroom before drinking it. Kelsey watches me curiously.

"I don't have much time," I tell her, getting comfy on the bed.

"Oh, where's your key, so I can lock up if I leave?" she asks.

I relax down into the pillows. "On the side table near the door. I'll see you later."

I close my eyes and wait.

Woo—okay, here we go!

EIGHT

I wake up in my old shower. It's a shock to show up randomly, wet, and naked. I'll have to remember that I won't always know where I am if I don't time my arrival for early in the morning.

I quickly finish bathing and step out, wrapping myself up in a towel. Why was I having a shower in the middle of the afternoon anyway?

Kelsey is sitting on my bed, flicking through a Cosmopolitan magazine. I jump with surprise.

"Are you all right, babe?" she asks.

"Yeah, sorry. I just forgot you were here."

"Weirdo. So...I've been asking around about Aaron—I called Rachel and asked her to find out from Chris where he might be this afternoon. Apparently, he's going to be in Maroochydore around five."

"So, you want to go down there?"

"Duh, of course. Why else would I be telling you?"

I remember what Kelsey said about wishing she hadn't spent so much time pining after Aaron back at school. "Are you sure you want to focus all that energy on finding the guy?"

"Come on, Anna! He's a total fox. And I know he's got a sweet side in there somewhere. He's just good at hiding it so his friends don't give him a hard time."

I want to tell her that she is sorely disappointed in the future. "What if he's anti-feminist?" I point out.

She laughs. "What? You think he wishes women stayed at home, chained to the kitchen sink?"

"You should ask him and find out."

"Maybe I will."

I go over to my cupboard to look for some clothes and decide on a grungy floral dress with my Docs. "When do you want to go?"

"I guess whenever you're dressed. We could already be there if you hadn't spilled half a bottle of Sun-In on you before."

"Oh. Sorry." So that explains the shower. I do vaguely remember that happening, now that she mentions it. It's funny how certain memories are stronger than others.

"Did you ask your mum if we could take the car?"

"Um…" Damn it. Did I do that before my shower? "I forgot. Hang on."

I quickly put my clothes on while Kelsey continues flicking through her magazine and go downstairs. I find Mum at the dining table, writing something on a notepad.

"Hey, is it okay if Kelsey and I borrow the car?" I ask.

She looks at me like I've grown another head. "Are you asking again because you didn't like the answer the first time?"

"Oh, no. I just couldn't remember if I had actually asked you, or if I thought I had."

"Nice try. The answer is still no."

I'm assuming she told me the reason before, so I won't push it by asking why.

"No problem." I hurry back up the stairs.

"Sorry, Mum won't let us use the car."

Kelsey's face drops. "That sucks."

"We can't use your car?" I ask.

"No. Mum banned me from driving it for three months after I dented the bumper."

"Do you think she'd mind if *I* drove it?"

"Anna, I'm surprised at you. Trying to circumvent the system." She smiles devilishly. "But I think you may have found a loophole. Mum loves you, and I'm sure she'd forgive you if she found out you drove her car. Which hopefully she won't. Do you think your mum could drop us at my place?"

"I can ask."

I just hope whatever reason she gave for not letting *me* use the car doesn't affect *her* ability to drive us anywhere.

"Is this your way of getting out of paying for petrol?" Mum asks when I find her again.

"Oh, no." I rummage around in my purse and find a twenty. I shove it in her face. "Here. Will that cover it?"

She looks at me, bemused. "Fine," she sighs. "But just this once."

We head out to the car and strap ourselves in the back.

"Where's your mum this afternoon?" I whisper to Kelsey.

"Her sister came and picked her up. They're heading to the club later to play bingo."

"Oh. Exciting. Not."

"I know. But that's good for us, because she'll probably be drunk when she gets home and not notice that me or the car is missing. Not that she cares," she says under her breath.

"Your mum cares about you!" I protest.

"I don't think she does. She's always so wrapped up in her own life that she barely pays attention to me. Do you know she forgot my birthday this year?"

I have a vague recollection of that happening. At the time, I didn't think much of it, but now as an adult, I can't understand how parents can just ignore their kids. Even if I don't have any of my own, I still see how much children rely on their parents to feel safe and nurtured.

"I remember you saying," I offer gently. "There's no excuse for that."

"And Andy has been acting really weird lately. He's put, like, five deadbolts on his bedroom door and never lets anyone in. Mum's threatened to remove the whole door, but he said he'd kill her if she did. And I wouldn't put it past him."

"Jeez, Kelsey. You poor thing. Is he going to be at home this afternoon?"

"Probably not. He usually goes out during the day. Hopefully, he won't be back until much later."

"Maybe you could come and stay at our place for a while?"

I'm not sure why I'm offering, since I won't be around to see it through, but it feels like the right thing to say.

She sighs. "Maybe. But it's not like I can move in with your family permanently. I'll have to go back eventually." She raises her voice a little. "You don't want an additional family member, do you Mrs. Parnell?"

Mum laughs. "Kelsey, I would love to have you stay with us, but I'm not sure your mother would allow it. Besides, I don't think you or Anna would cope being stuck together twenty-four seven."

Actually, that's true. Kelsey always thought I was too square. I hope it doesn't become an issue when we work together.

We reach her house and jump out. "Thanks, Mum," I say, feeling every bit the teenager I look.

"Don't be home too late."

"I won't." It's easier for the moment to agree than tell her I have no intention of returning home tonight. If she calls later, I'll just text her and let her know I decided to stay at Kelsey's. "Bye!"

We wait until she drives away before Kelsey runs inside to retrieve her mum's car keys. I wait in the carport beside their old Ford Falcon.

"This is awesome! I feel like Thelma and Louise!" she squeals, coming back out and unlocking the doors.

"As long as we don't end up like them."

She cackles. "Don't worry, I don't have a death wish or anything."

"I'm glad to hear it." I hesitate before climbing in the car. I just remembered I need to ask about the memento tin. "Kelsey?"

"What?"

"I was thinking of making a time capsule. What do you think?"

"Really?"

"Yeah. We could write letters to ourselves and put some keepsakes in there...maybe photos of the boys we liked..."

She looks conflicted. "I guess..."

"Don't you think it would be fun?"

She seems to internally debate something. "The thing is...I kind of already buried all my keepsakes."

"Oh."

"I'm sorry, I didn't think it would ever come up. It was late one night, and I was mad at Andy because he'd threatened to trash my room, so I put all my favourite things in a tin and buried it in the bush behind the house here."

"Could you maybe dig it up and add some of my stuff to it?"

"I don't know...or you could just do your own?"

"Could I bury it near yours? There are no good places near my house."

"If you really want to..."

"Yes, please. Can we do it now?"

"What? You mean go back to your place and get the stuff and come back?"

"Yes?"

"That will take forever! I want to go to Maroochydore and find Aaron before it gets too late. How about I just quickly show you where my spot is and then you can come back later? As long as you promise to leave my stuff alone."

"Of course I promise."

"All right." We trudge around the side of her house and into the bush. "What's the hurry anyway?"

"I don't know. I was watching *Back to the Future* the other day and it got me thinking…" I'm getting pretty good at making up all this stuff on the spot.

"I love that movie! Number two is way better than number one, though, don't you think?"

"Definitely."

"I wonder how different everything will be in 2015?"

"Not like the movie. But I think there will be some cool technology."

"You're probably right. I hope they have those machines that look like microwaves that cook a whole meal in a few seconds."

"Me, too," I say, playing along.

I'm grateful she doesn't ask any further questions. I'm not in the mood to do the whole reveal thing again. Once in the past and once in the future is more than enough.

We head into the bush and walk in a straight line for a couple of minutes. I make a note of the trees and rocks around us, but there aren't many identifying features.

"Aren't you worried you're going to forget the spot?" I ask.

"Nah. Look." She points to a small formation of rocks. "It's right near here. The rock in the middle is shaped like a heart."

I look at the rock and see what she means. I mentally commit it to memory.

She stops beside a large gum tree.

"Here," she says. "I buried it halfway between this tree and those rocks."

"Cool. Thank you for sharing your secret spot with me."

"I guess we'll have to organise a special ceremony in twenty years for the official re-opening."

"That would be fun. Book it in."

She looks up at the sky. "Can we go now? It's getting late."

"Sure."

We walk back towards her house and get in her mum's car. Kelsey puts a cassette in the player and Savage Garden's *I Want You* blares out. She turns it down a little and starts telling me about her plans to capture Aaron's attention.

"Have you ever considered just being normal?" I suggest as we drive down the coast road.

She wrinkles her nose. "Where's the fun in that? I want him to be intrigued! To become obsessed with me."

"But is he worth it?"

"Yes. He is."

I don't say anything. It's not like anything I say now will change the real future.

"So, do you know where he's going to be in Maroochydore?"

"Just somewhere at The Palace."

"You mean you don't know his exact location?"

"Nope," she says cheerfully. "But that's all part of the fun."

"If you say so."

When we reach The Palace, we park the car and head inside.

"Where do you want to start?" I ask.

"I think maybe HMV."

HMV used to be a huge music store on the top floor of the mall. I'd totally forgotten about it, but now that Kelsey has reminded me, I recall spending many an afternoon there. It was less intimidating than Kurt's shop across the road.

I wonder if he's working…

Inside HMV, Kelsey starts acting like a lunatic.

"Play it cool," I laugh as she races around the aisles, inspecting every customer in the store.

After thirty seconds, she looks at me, crestfallen. "He's not here."

"That's okay. There are lots of other places to search."

"You're right. Let's go down to the food court. Maybe he's eating."

Downstairs, it's pretty busy with the early dinner crowd. I involuntarily look up to the seating area where I met Maddie. It feels like a lifetime ago now. Sometimes I wonder if I hadn't tracked Ed down in 1996 whether we'd still be together now. Or if we would have eventually split up anyway.

Kelsey fixes her gaze on every person in the food court. "He's not here, either," she moans.

"Maybe we should just do our own thing. Don't they have a saying about finding something once you stop looking?"

"I don't believe that. I feel like this was supposed to be easy. Like I'd know exactly where to find him because we're meant to be together."

"Babe, don't beat yourself up about it. You're not psychic. And just because you can't predict where he'll be doesn't mean you're not supposed to be together."

If only she knew she'll eventually get her wish, and she'll regret it.

"I guess we could go look at some clothes and then grab something from McDonald's," she says.

"If you like." I'm happy to just go with the flow for the rest of the evening. I've already mostly achieved my objective. And while I'd like to see Kurt, I'd feel kind of bad manipulating the situation when this visit was for Kelsey's benefit. I should stay with her.

We trawl through the racks in the youth clothing boutiques and then head up to Target. Even there, the grunge theme is prevalent.

We pick out a few outfits each and try them on in the changing rooms. I know I won't be able to enjoy them after tonight, but I'm starting to appreciate that even in the future, all we have is the current moment. Nothing lasts forever. It's just that my time here is a bit shorter, and I have no one to talk about it with later—unless you count Kelsey, which I don't, yet. That should make it even more special, really.

After buying matching red plaid skirts and black ribbed shirts, we head over to McDonald's. In the future, I love the familiarity of stopping in at McDonald's wherever I go, because I know I can rely on it to have the same menu and vibe every time. It's the same here in the past.

We order quarter pounders and Cokes and sit down facing the window.

Kelsey nibbles at her burger before putting it down.

"Do you think I'm crazy?" she asks. "For being obsessed with a guy who barely even knows I exist?"

"Maybe just leave your options open," I say gently.

"Yeah. That's probably a good idea."

"Do you have anyone else in mind?"

"No." She looks out the window mournfully.

And then she sees something that obviously makes her happy.

"Ooh. But I like him."

I follow her gaze.

Of course.

It's Kurt.

NINE

My heart starts hammering. Every part of me wants to run out there and throw my arms around him, but I manage to restrain myself. Just.

Kurt comes to a standstill outside the restaurant and starts looking through his wallet.

"I...uh...I know him," I say casually.

"You do?" Kelsey shrieks. "Introduce me!"

"I can't. He won't remember who I am. But his name is Kurt, and he works at the record store around the corner."

She jumps up. "That's enough for me."

"Kelsey! Wait."

She ignores me and bounds out of McDonald's, cornering Kurt just as he's putting his wallet back in his pocket.

He looks up politely as she talks to him. I don't know what she's saying, but he doesn't look too freaked out. It should have occurred to me that this situation may arise in one of our realities. Of course I understand that Kelsey would also be attracted to Kurt. He's pretty hard not to be attracted to.

I pile our half-finished meals back into their paper bags and balance the two Cokes on top as I carry them outside.

Kelsey's eyes are shining. "I was just saying to Kurt how I saw him at the record store the other day and how I need his music knowledge to figure out what to play at my party next weekend." She gives me a pointed look as if to say *just go along with it.*

I nod. "Right."

Kurt focuses on me for a second.

"Hey, you look really familiar," he says.

I hide a smile. That never gets old. And if only I could tell him we got *very familiar* last weekend.

"Anna said she knew you, but you probably wouldn't know her. Maybe you recognise her from when she went into your shop?"

He continues to study me. "Maybe. I feel like it was somewhere else, though."

"Either way, do you think you can help?"

He looks at his watch. "Actually, I was just about to meet my cousin, Chris, who is down here with some buddies. We were going to see a movie in half an hour. But I guess you could hang with us until then?" He gives me a look I can't interpret.

Kelsey doesn't notice. She's launched into heavy-duty flirting mode. I wonder how she'll feel when she realises that Chris is Rachel's brother. Who also happens to be friends with Aaron.

"Perfect." She forces Kurt to loop his arm through hers. I'm stuck still holding our food.

"Lead the way," she purrs.

I shouldn't be jealous, but I find it a bit frustrating that Kelsey has changed her allegiances so quickly—and with Kurt of all people. I know I don't really have a claim on him, but after everything we've gone through, it's hard not to feel a bit put out.

"I'm just meeting the guys outside the cinema," he says. He then notices me lugging all the food. He takes the drinks from me before I can protest. "You can't carry all that stuff on your own."

"Thank you," I say gratefully.

"So, what kind of music do you like?" Kurt asks Kelsey.

"Oh, a fair bit. Chili Peppers…Nirvana…Pearl Jam…"

"All good bands, but Nirvana and Pearl Jam aren't exactly upbeat if you're after a party vibe."

"True. What do you recommend?"

"Maybe Faithless? Or CJ Bolland? Robert Miles?"

"See, I knew you were the right person to ask," she simpers.

I'd forgotten what Kelsey was like in attack mode. Kurt better watch out.

"What kind of stuff are *you* into?" Kurt asks me.

I am *so* tempted to mention *Sad-Eyed Lady of the Lowlands*, but I know that would be playing dirty.

"Um, actually I like a bit of everything. Even Shaggy." Ha.

He laughs. "There's nothing wrong with a bit of pop music. Don't tell anyone at work I said this, but I'm a bit of a Shaggy fan myself."

"Your secret's safe with us," Kelsey assures him.

We reach the cinema, and Chris is sitting on a picnic bench, smoking a cigarette. And it's as I suspected. Aaron is also with them.

Kelsey sees him immediately and drops her arm from Kurt's. She runs over.

"Aaron! What a surprise! I didn't expect to see you here!"

He eyes her warily. "Hey, Kelsey."

Kurt looks at me. "You know these guys?"

"Yeah, Chris's sister goes to school with us."

"Oh. Cool. Maybe that's where I've seen you before—around Shell Beach when I've been visiting Chris."

That's not it.

"That's maybe it," I agree.

Kelsey has now very clearly set her tractor beam back on Aaron. Kurt seems bemused by the whole situation. He leans against a nearby wall.

"You mind if I have a sip of your drink?" he asks, indicating the two containers he's still holding.

"Oh, sure. Go ahead."

"Which one's yours?" he asks, eyes twinkling.

"Ah, that one," I say pointing to the one on the left.

I watch to see if he goes for the one on the right instead. He hesitates for a second, as if pretending to consider which one to drink, and then takes a long pull on mine.

My skin tingles. Part of me hates that we have to meet all over again every time I come back here, but the other part loves that we get to flirt as if for the first time over and over.

"You going to finish eating?" he asks.

"Oh, yeah." I slide down and sit with my back against the wall beside Kurt. He joins me on the ground.

"Your friend is fun," he says mildly. We both watch as she entertains Chris and Aaron by folding her tongue into a weird shape.

"Kelsey's great. A little wacky, but we balance each other out."

"I'll bet."

"What were you guys seeing tonight?"

"Uh, *Romeo and Juliet*. The guys aren't super psyched about it, but I like Baz Luhrmann, and I heard the soundtrack is decent."

"Cool."

"Have you already seen it?"

Yes. Like a million times once it went to video.

"No, I haven't. I've read a positive review of it, though."

"Hey, if you two aren't doing anything else, did you maybe want to come and see it with us?"

He seems nervous asking. How adorable.

I look over at Kelsey, who now has one of her hands pressed against Aaron's and is cooing over how much bigger his is. He laughs nervously.

"Kelsey? Do you want to see the movie, too?"

She looks like she might pass out from the excitement. "Yes!"

Aaron shoots Kurt a thanks-a-lot expression. Kurt shrugs and smiles.

"It's all settled, then. When you finish your food, we'll head inside."

"Do you want the rest of your stuff?" I ask Kelsey.

She looks over and wrinkles her nose. "No, thanks."

I try not to roll my eyes. I'd forgotten how intense she used to get around Aaron.

"Do you mind if I eat it?" Kurt asks her.

"Go for it."

He opens up her half-eaten burger, which to be honest, doesn't look that great, and munches beside me.

"So, Anna. Tell me something about you. Apart from your obsession with Shaggy."

I laugh. "I thought we'd established that *you* were the one with the Shaggy obsession. But anyway, I like to cook. Or bake, I guess."

"What's your signature recipe?"

"A raspberry frangipane tart. And in case you're wondering, frangipane is an almond-flavoured pastry cream."

"Wow. That sounds awesome. You'll have to make it for me sometime."

I would love to. But it's probably not going to happen unless I make it tonight.

I glance over at Kelsey. She's drinking directly from a wine bottle that's materialised out of nowhere.

"Do you drink?" Kurt asks, nodding at the bottle.

"A little. Not much."

"You're not eighteen yet, are you?"

Yes.

"No."

"I would offer to buy you something, but it doesn't quite feel right."

"It's okay. I don't need you to buy me anything."

"You seem a lot more chilled out than most girls your age."

"Thank you."

I want to tell him that he's the reason I'm so chilled out. That I would be happy anywhere he is—even sitting on the pavement outside a cinema eating McDonald's.

"All right, I suppose we should go in," Aaron says. He doesn't look like he's excited at all now that Kelsey has glued herself to his side.

Kurt stands up and takes my empty food packaging, putting it in a nearby bin. I follow him and the others inside to line up for tickets.

"I'll buy," Kurt says to me.

"No, don't be silly. I can afford it."

"That's not why I offered."

"But…"

"But nothing. Just let me buy you a damn ticket."

I smile. "Okay. Thank you."

Kurt purchases two tickets and hands me one. We then all troop into the cinema and sit down. It's a slightly awkward affair determining who sits where. Kelsey clearly won't sit down unless she's beside Aaron. Finally, she sits on one end, and Aaron sits next to her. Chris sits next to him, and Kurt sits down next. I plop down next to him at the other end. I guess Kelsey doesn't need me for company. To be honest, I didn't want to watch her mauling Aaron anyway.

I'm hyper-aware of my presence next to Kurt. It's as if there's a continuous invisible lightning storm in the few inches between us.

I was more than happy to make tonight about Kelsey, but she went and made it about Aaron and Kurt. I'm definitely not complaining.

Who says you can't have your cake and eat it, too?

TEN

It takes Kurt half the film to work up the courage to put his arm around the back of my seat. I smile stupidly in the dark. It was never like this with Ed, even in the beginning. Somehow, we skipped all the nervousness and flirting and went straight to a sensible adult relationship.

A tiny part of me feels bad for misrepresenting myself. I mean, if Kurt knew how old I really was, he'd probably run a mile. Also, I'm sure it's not normal for someone my age to be obsessed with a twenty-three-year-old.

But there's something about the two of us that just works. Age doesn't feel like an issue when we're together.

By the end of the film, which I don't actually pay much attention to, Kurt is resting his arm on my shoulder. I have snuggled in close and can breathe in his scent. He's wearing that same sandalwood cologne I remember from the night on the beach.

I wonder if Kelsey is having as nice a time as me. I glance over. She does not look happy and is sitting with her arms crossed in front of her.

The credits roll, and she jumps up. She pushes her way past the three guys dividing us and grabs my hand.

"Come on, Anna, let's go."

She doesn't seem to have noticed how cosy Kurt and I are.

Kurt stands up and tries to follow us out, but Kelsey blocks him.

"I'm sorry, Kurt, but I need my girl right now."

He holds up his hands in surrender. "That's cool," he says, his eyes not matching his actions and words.

"Can I at least get your number?" he asks me.

"Sure." I scribble it down on a piece of paper from my purse and hand it over. I mouth the word *sorry* to him and hurry out to keep up with Kelsey. I'm not pleased with how quickly my time with Kurt has been cut short, but at least I know none of this will matter in a few hours anyway.

"What happened in there?" I ask.

She angrily wipes tears away from her eyes.

"He's a bastard," she hisses.

"Why?"

"He wouldn't even damn well touch me. Acted like I was a leper."

"Oh. I'm sorry, Kels. Maybe the timing just isn't right. And like we talked about before, maybe it's best you keep your options open."

We walk back to the car, Kelsey whimpering quietly. I miss Kurt, but I try and see this as an opportunity to comfort my best friend over the disappointment of a man who lets her down again in the future. I wasn't around when her marriage to Aaron ended, so I can sort of make up for it now.

"Do you want to stop and get ice cream sundaes on the way home?" I ask.

"I'm not hungry."

"What if we stay up all night and watch the Top 40?"

"I don't know. I'm kind of tired."

"Do you want me to go home?"

"No, no. You can do whatever. Stay or don't stay."

"All right. We'll see how you feel when we get back to your place."

We drive back to Shell Beach in silence. Kelsey's mum and Andy are still out, so we make ourselves comfortable in the living room. Kelsey raids the liquor cabinet and pours us large glasses of rum and Coke, heavy on the rum.

She gulps her drink down in record time and winces. "I need to forget about tonight." And then something seems to occur to her.

"Oh, shit, babe. Did I totally ruin your night with Kurt?"

I laugh. "You're only just figuring that out now?"

"God, I did, didn't I? I am the worst friend in the world."

"You're not. It's fine."

Something else seems to click in her brain.

"I totally tried to steal him from you, too, huh?"

"You can't steal someone."

"No, but you said you already knew him, and I didn't even think to ask more about that."

My mobile starts ringing and Kelsey squeals. "I bet that's him!" She snatches the phone out of my hand and clicks the *Answer* key before I have a chance to react.

"Hello?" she says. "This is Anna's phone."

A beat.

"Oh, hi, Kurt. Yeah, we're just chilling at my house. At Shell Beach."

She's quiet while he says something.

"Of course. Do you have a pen?"

I frantically wave my hands at her. She ignores me.

"It's 34 Seamist Drive."

Another beat.

"Perfect. See you soon!"

She hangs up and cackles gleefully. "He's coming here to see you! Now!"

"You didn't have to do that."

"Yes, I did. To make up for my appalling behaviour earlier." She gulps down the rest of her drink. "Come on, finish yours. I'll make us another one."

"I'll be drunk," I warn.

"That's what I'm counting on," she teases. "I don't want you getting all nervous around Kurt."

I think it's sweet she's trying to redeem herself, but I'm not feeling nervous at all. Just excited.

"Are you hoping he brings Aaron?"

"Oh, no. I hope he doesn't. Chris is okay, but I'm over Aaron now."

"What? In half an hour?"

"That's right."

"Well, good for you."

"And the least I can do is make sure *someone* is happy today."

"That's very sweet of you."

She takes my glass out of my hand. "Let me do your makeup."

"Why?"

"So Kurt won't be able to resist you when he arrives."

"I don't want to look like I'm trying too hard."

"I promise you won't."

She drags me upstairs to her room and surveys my face. After a moment, she retrieves the bag of cosmetics she keeps in her bedside cabinet and starts expertly painting my skin with foundation, blending it in and adding some tasteful eyeshadow. She plucks my eyebrows, which need tidying up again, and sorts out my eyelashes. She paints my lips with a peachy gloss and smiles at her handiwork.

I sneak a peek in the mirror and beam.

"You are so good at this. You should be a professional makeup artist."

"No way. I want to be a millionaire. You know I'm planning a career as a fashion designer."

I don't have time to rehash our previous conversation about the industry, so I just smile.

There's a knock at the door.

Kelsey squeals. "He's here!"

"You seem more excited than I am," I observe.

"I'm just happy I got to make up for my poor form before." She points to the stairs. "Go on, you answer the door. I'll be down in a minute."

"Okay."

I walk down the stairs, feeling very much like a giddy teenager, and open the door.

Kurt is standing there, smiling.

"Hey," I say.

He steps forward. "Before we go any further, I need to do this." He cups my face and kisses me gently. I almost swoon.

"I'm...I'm glad you felt the need to do that," I say breathlessly afterwards.

"I didn't think I'd be able to sleep tonight unless I did."

"Well, we couldn't have that."

Kelsey bounds down the stairs and into the living room. "Hey, Kurt! Welcome to my humble abode. Come in!"

"Actually, I know this is really uncool, but do you mind if I just have a quick chat to Anna outside? I can't stay long."

"Oh, sure. No problem. Hey, what do you think of my handiwork? I want to be a makeup artist, so I was practicing on Anna."

Kurt studies my face for a moment. "I'd say you have a pretty good model to work with, but well done."

I blush.

"Okay, I'll just be inside if you need me," Kelsey says. She winks at me as she disappears.

"Sorry about her," I say as we go out onto the driveway. "She felt bad about…" I trail off.

"Getting in our way earlier?" he finishes.

"I mean, I don't think I have more of a chance with you than Kelsey or anything…"

He cuts me off. "Trust me, you do. I don't know what it is, but it's like…I don't know. Like the stars have aligned especially for us?" He laughs. "Sorry, that even sounded cheesy in my brain."

"It's not cheesy. I feel the same."

He strokes my cheek. "I know it's late, so I won't keep you, but I had to see you once more tonight so I could say goodbye properly."

"I'm glad you came."

He pulls my face to his and kisses me again. His lips are so soft. I lose myself in his mouth as he opens up and gently brushes his tongue over mine. I wonder if my teenage hormones have anything to do with how incredibly good this feels.

But it doesn't seem to be just me reacting this way. "Oh God," Kurt groans. "What are you doing to me?"

I smile and nip his neck and earlobe. "I don't know, but I wouldn't question it."

He fixes his gaze on me, and our noses are almost touching. "I really do feel like I've known you forever."

"I know what you mean," I murmur.

"Can I join the party?" an unwelcome voice slurs behind us. I jump back. It's Andy.

"Uh, no. We were just leaving."

"Aw, come on. I haven't gotten laid in forever."

Kurt puts himself between me and Andy. "Look, I don't know who you are, but it's disrespectful to Anna to talk like that."

"I don't give a fuck what you think, buddy. You're on my property."

"Not for much longer." Kurt grips my hand tightly and pulls me onto the street. "Come on, Anna."

I don't argue.

***

As we hurry over to Kurt's car, I see him keeping an eye on Andy, who stands at the top of the driveway, watching us leave.

Kurt opens the door for me. He has an old Holden HR station wagon. It's immaculately restored and painted pale green with a white roof.

"This is a very cool car," I say when Kurt climbs into the driver's seat.

"I like it," he agrees. He starts the motor, and we roar off down the road. "Who the hell was that creep? He's not related to Kelsey, is he?"

"Yeah, he's her brother. And he's worse than you think."

"I'm not sure if that's even possible."

"Thank you for being my knight in shining armour," I joke, fluttering my eyelashes at him.

"I have a feeling you can stand up for yourself, Anna."

"I can, but it's nice to have someone else for support."

"I should have checked if you were comfortable leaving with me, but I didn't like the idea of you being in the same house as him."

"No, I didn't much like that idea either."

"What do you want to do? Do you want me to take you home?"

"Uh, I'm not sure yet. Can we just drive around for a bit? As long as you're not too tired?"

"I'm not tired. I'm kind of a night owl. I only told Kelsey I couldn't stay long because I didn't want to look like I expected anything from you."

"Such a gentleman," I tease.

He drives us over to near Main Street and up to a nearby lookout. I jump out of the car and lean against the railing, quietly taking in the view of the coast and all the surrounding houses. Kurt comes up behind me and wraps his arms around my waist, resting his chin on the top of my head.

"This town is beautiful," he says.

"It is."

He repositions himself so he can see my face. "Would it be super corny if I now say, 'but not as beautiful as you?'"

"A little. But it's okay. I'll allow it."

He laughs. "Good."

"What do you think you'll be doing in twenty years?" I ask suddenly.

He seems to take my question seriously. "Um, I don't know. I hope I'm doing something I love, and spending time with someone I love. I guess that's all anyone can ask for, really. What about you?"

"I think I'll do pretty good career-wise. Maybe be married…" I don't say that I'll also have just divorced.

"What about kids? Do you want kids?"

"Possibly. I don't know. I'm not sure I'm into the idea of children. You?"

"I want a huge family. Maybe six or seven kids."

I burst out laughing. "What? Really?"

He winks. "No. But I do want at least a couple. I love the idea of being a dad.

My heart almost melts inside my chest. I lean over and kiss him again.

"Is that your pick-up line?" I ask, smiling.

"Um, you might not have noticed, but I've already picked you up."

"Or is it your 'get the girl into bed' line?"

"Hey, I don't need any lines to get a girl into bed. My natural charisma does that for me."

I know he's being silly, but I have to agree. "There *is* something about you."

"So why don't you want kids?" he asks.

"I don't know. I guess I don't want to be tied down."

"Is that the only reason?"

He's very perceptive. "I guess it depends on the guy I end up with. He might not want them either."

His face falls for a second. "That's true."

"Oh God, sorry. I didn't mean I was thinking about some other random person right now."

Unless you count my experience with my ex-husband.

"It's okay. It's true that the likelihood of us being together in twenty years is small. And I know we've only known each other for a few hours, and I don't want to sound like a stalker…so I'm just going to shut up now."

I giggle. "You're so cute when you're nervous."

"I'm not nervous. Okay, maybe you make me a little nervous."

"Do I?"

"Yes, you do."

He leans over and kisses me again, this time slowly making his way down to the top of my chest. I'm just wondering whether he's going to push aside the fabric of my dress when a pair of very bright headlights shine on us.

We both jump back.

"I think that was a reminder for me to slow things down," he says, chuckling.

I pout. I don't want him to slow things down.

"You're too nice for your own good."

He grins. "I can be bad when I want to be. Come on, let me take you home. I wouldn't want your mum to worry about you."

"Okay."

We hop back in the car.

"You want to pick an album to listen to?" he asks, pointing to the glovebox.

I open it and see a bunch of cassettes. I turn the overheard light on and flick through them.

"You didn't want to get a record player fitted in here?" I joke. "Because it would sound better?"

"Uh, I think all the records would get scratched every time I went over a bump," he shoots back.

"You might have a point there."

I pick out Massive Attack's *Protection* album and slot it into the player.

"Good choice," he says, hearing the intro.

I'm just about to close the glovebox again when I see some paperwork folded up in the corner. I pull it out.

"Oh, that's just the rego," he says. "Nothing exciting."

I look at the name. "Kurt Hamilton."

"That's me. What's your surname?"

"Parnell."

"Anna Parnell." He rolls the words around on his tongue. "I like it."

I direct Kurt back to my house, where he stops across the street.

"Thank you for tonight, Anna."

"No, thank *you*."

"Can I call you tomorrow?"

Only if your phone can call through time.

"Sure."

He kisses me one last time, and I savour every moment.

When I get out of the car, I'm floating on air. I wave to Kurt and walk up my driveway. I have no intention of going inside, so I pretend to fumble with my keys until he leaves.

Once I'm sure he's gone, I call a cab.

I'm going to be finishing this journey to 1997 somewhere else tonight.

ELEVEN

In the cab, I get out of my phone and see I have two missed calls. I phone into voicemail.

The first message is from Mum.

"Anna, I was just wondering what time you planned on coming home? Your father and I are going to bed soon, and you know we hate not knowing where you are."

I skip to the next message.

"Hey babe, I hope you're having fun. I spoke to Andy, and by the sounds of it, he was a total dick to you, so I'm sorry, and I understand why you left. If you come back later, just climb up the balcony and knock on the door. But otherwise, enjoy your grunge god!"

I smile. Kelsey is the best. I quickly text Mum my excuse about staying at Kelsey's and switch off the phone. I'm not actually outright lying, because I have the driver take me back to her house, but instead of going inside, I borrow a shovel and flashlight from inside the carport and head back into the bush we visited earlier.

It's a little creepy here at night. The trees rustle in the breeze, but otherwise it's quiet, and my footsteps sound really loud crunching over the ground.

It takes a bit longer than I expected, but I finally spy the mound of rocks and the gum tree we stopped at earlier.

I find what I hope is the middle and dig my shovel in. The ground is quite sandy, so I'm fortunate that I don't have to exert too much energy.

The problem is, I don't know how deep Kelsey buried the box, or if I'm even in the correct place. Knowing my bestie, she wouldn't have buried it too deep.

I work for about fifteen minutes, piling the sandy soil beside me. I can't imagine what a passing spectator might think. I probably look like I'm disposing of a dead body.

Just when I'm about to give up, my shovel hits something hard and metallic. I reach down and use my fingers to dig it out of the ground.

It's an old shortbread tin. I pry it open and smile. Bingo.

Kelsey has lined the tin with plastic, and inside is a bunch of photos and other bits and pieces. I sit down and position the light so I can look at everything properly.

Apart from the photos, there's a rose quartz crystal in the shape of a heart, a troll doll keyring, a bracelet made of brightly coloured plastic beads, a cassette with *90s mix tape* written on the label, and a folded piece of paper. I unfold it and read Kelsey's messy scrawl.

Hi Future Kelsey,

Hopefully by the time you read this, you will be a mega successful fashion designer and married to Aaron.

You will have an awesome penthouse in Brisbane overlooking the water, and you will be driving a red BMW convertible. You will be thinking of starting a family, but you don't want kids too early. You need to travel around the world first.

Also, you will still be best friends with Anna, and the two of you will have awesome adventures.

Kelsey.

P.S. If you ever figure out how to time travel, come back and say hi. I promise I won't tell anyone, and I'll play it totally cool!

I smile and fold it back up, putting it in the tin with the other items. At least I can vouch for the fact that she did handle the original time-travel revelation in 1996 quite well.

I've left the photos until last.

The first one is a picture of Aaron, cut from our school yearbook. On the back in hot pink ink are the words *my future husband*. Well, she got that right.

The second photo is one of Kelsey with her family. I never met her dad, because he left when she was five. This picture shows a man with thick curly black hair standing beside Kelsey's mum, and a young, but surly looking Andy beside her. A four-year-old Kelsey is beaming at the camera. It's such a shame how things turned out for her family.

The last picture is of her and I. It was taken down at Shell Beach in the middle of summer. We're both wearing matching pink bikinis and pouting at the camera. I turn over the photo. The words on the back say *best friends forever* with a heart.

At least we're back together now in the present.

I put the photos on top of everything else and seal up the tin. I put it back in the hole and pile the dirt over it. It's much faster doing this part.

I'm quite sweaty when I'm finished, and very, very tired. I lie down on top of my newly flattened patch of ground and close my eyes.

I don't think I can stay awake until 3am.

***

I open my eyes, still feeling the echo of the Shell Beach breeze.

"You look satisfied," Kelsey's wry voice says. "I take it your little trip went well?"

"Yup."

"Well, you freaked me out, even though I thought I knew what to expect. You basically went into a coma. At one point, I swear your pulse stopped. I was *this* close to calling an ambulance."

"I'm glad you didn't." I sit up. "So, you tried to wake me up?"

"Yes. I yelled in your face, and I pinched your arm. At first, I thought you were pranking me, trying to stretch out the act for as long as you could, but then I knew you couldn't be *that* good at acting. Thank God you woke up this morning."

I stand up and head to the kitchen to heat up some water for tea.

"Well, I can prove once and for all I'm not lying," I tell her.

"What? You actually found my tin?"

"That's right. In the bush behind your house at Shell Beach. Between a large gum tree and a pile of rocks. One of them was shaped like a heart. You put your stuff in a shortbread tin…some photos, a letter to yourself, and a few trinkets, like a rose quartz crystal and a troll doll keyring."

Her face goes white. "Holy shit."

"Do you believe me now?"

She slowly sits down on the edge of the couch. "Oh my God."

I look at her, concerned. "Are you all right?"

"I…just…I really thought this was all a big joke."

"It's not."

"Clearly."

"So, would you like to try it?"

She sits there, dazed for a moment, and then looks at me.

"Yes. Now. Before I chicken out."

"Can you afford to lose a whole day?"

"Babe, I wouldn't care if my mother was scheduled to have life-saving surgery. Okay, that's probably going a bit far, but you know what I mean. This is a chance to go back in time!"

"You want me to go back, too?"

"Yeah, I think so. I'd feel better knowing you were going through the same thing, even if we end up in different realities. You need to explore this shit. For scientific purposes."

I laugh. "Well, when you put it that way...actually, I haven't been very scientific so far. Apart from discovering Ed and Maddie's mutual obsession, my main priorities have been visiting my grandma and..."

"Grandma Millie?" Kelsey cuts in. "I know you told me yesterday, but that was before I knew you were telling me the truth. Didn't your grandma die forever ago?"

I nod sadly. "It's been so nice to see her again, but also hard knowing that I can't visit her here now."

"Wow. I can't get my head around the idea of seeing people who died."

"Or people that you never met the first time around," I add.

"What do you mean?"

"I...uh...I kind of keep running into this guy called Kurt..."

"Go on..."

"And even though he doesn't remember me every time I go back, we always seem to reconnect. Last night, you actually saw him first."

Kelsey looks a little overwhelmed. "Hang on. Why doesn't he remember you?"

"You know how I told you each visit stands alone? That means if you didn't meet someone in the real 1997, they won't know who you are the next time you go back."

"My head hurts."

"It's best not to worry about the logistics too much."

"I'm torn between wanting to know more about this Kurt guy, but also wanting to just take the stuff and see what happens. Hopefully, we wake up in the same place and you can keep explaining everything as we go."

"Fingers crossed! All right. You ready?"

"As I'll ever be."

I go to the kitchen, get two glasses of water, and measure out two half teaspoons. I hand Kelsey one of the glasses.

"Why is it purple?"

"I don't know. It doesn't taste great, either."

"You go first."

"Sure." I encourage her to follow me with her drink into the bedroom. I gulp down mine and wince.

Kelsey looks at her glass as if contemplating whether to actually follow through and then shrugs. She downs it in one mouthful.

"I wonder if this is how Alice felt in Wonderland."

"It's a bit of a trip," I confirm. "Just relax. I'll see you either way soon."

TWELVE

I wake up, feeling that weird sense of déjà vu again. The old movie posters and CDs are scattered around the room. Kelsey is lying next to me. I gently tap her arm. "Hey. Wake up."

She groans. And then opens her eyes.

She sits bolt upright. "Holy shit."

I laugh delightedly. "You're here!"

She stares at me, her eyes wide. "Fuck! Anna! Is that you?"

"You mean the old-lady version of me? Yep."

She jumps out of bed and pounces on the mirror, not unlike my reaction when I first arrived last year.

"This is really happening."

"Well, sort of. Whatever *really* means."

"How have you not just been living here non-stop since you discovered this stuff?"

"I guess I didn't really know what it was at the beginning. And I only have thirty doses, so I didn't want to waste them. And after finding out about Ed…"

"Oh, of course. Wow! I love my body! I wish there was a way I could take it back with me!" She admires her stomach and legs in the mirror.

"Is there anything in particular you'd like to do?"

"I don't know. The possibilities are endless!" She races around, picking up the CDs and laughing. "Oh my God. I love it! And my posters!"

We hear shuffling in the hall, and Kelsey freezes. She tiptoes over and opens the door a crack, peeping through.

She closes it again and looks at me. "It's Andy."

I frown. "Great."

She suddenly looks stricken. "He hasn't been to jail yet. I have to stop him! Get him into counselling or something."

"You know that won't have any effect on the future," I say gently.

Her face falls. "Oh, right."

"But if this version does continue, it could make a difference here."

"Maybe."

After a moment, she shakes herself. "All right. I'll deal with that later. Let's get dressed and go out to explore."

I open the bag I had apparently brought over for the sleepover at her place. It contains yesterday's outfit, which is all crumpled up, and what I assume I brought for today—a purple suede skirt and a black top with an open back.

Kelsey flings open her wardrobe and examines the contents. "I feel like I'm on the set of a flashback movie. Look at this stuff!"

She holds up a pair of cherry-coloured Doc Martens. "I'm *so* wearing these today."

She pulls out a flowing blue dress with buttons up the middle and puts it on, spinning around. "I think I'm going to have to start wearing stuff like this again in the future."

"I know, right? Nineties fashion was fun."

"So, what now?"

"Do you want to talk to your mum or Andy?"

"Not really."

"Then I guess we could go out the usual way?" I look at the balcony.

"Let's do it."

We grab our bags and climb over the railing, using a nearby tree to assist our descent, and run off up the road, laughing. I have to admit, visiting the nineties with future Kelsey is a lot more fun than visiting on my own. And while I really liked spending time with the younger version of her, it's much easier with the one my own age.

"Let's go down to Main Street. Oh, do you think Jackson would be working?"

"I don't know. I guess we can find out."

We catch the bus to Beans, with Kelsey squealing every five seconds about how different everything is.

"Calm down, babe. You're going to freak out all the other passengers."

"I can't help it. This is so cool. You know, I had this idea once that when you die, you get access to your whole life and can relive any moment whenever you like. This is sort of the same. Only hopefully we're not dead."

"We're not dead."

"And obviously it's not a dream, otherwise we wouldn't be able to communicate this way."

"Yeah, I really don't know what it is. The only explanation I can come up with is that we're back in a real point in the past, but as soon as we do anything different, this reality breaks off into a parallel universe. But I don't know if it continues after we wake up or not."

"Who cares? Whatever happens next doesn't affect us!"

"I suppose…"

I still can't help feeling bad, though, for the possible Anna who had to deal with the aftermath of telling her mother she might be pregnant. Or waking up in random outdoor places. Would her brain somehow integrate the previous day's events as part of her own experience? Or would it be like she lost a whole twelve hours each time?

We arrive at Beans and go inside. Jackson is working.

"Hey!" Kelsey says brightly. "Wow. You look so different!"

I give her a warning look. She ignores me.

Jackson smiles, bemused. "In a good way?"

"Not in a good *or* bad way. Just different. You're a hottie now, but I know for a fact you're going to age really well, too."

He laughs. "Okaaayyy…for a fact, huh?"

"Never mind Kelsey," I say, pulling a comical face. "She's doing this roleplay thing where she's pretending to be psychic."

"Oh, right." He gives me a conspiratorial smile. "So, what does my future hold, Wise Kelsey?"

"You and I are going to live together in Brisbane in just over twenty years," she says cheerfully. "You're an awesome roomie."

"Is that so?"

"And you'll meet a very sweet guy called Cash. I think you'll probably get married."

He furrows a brow. "What?"

"Oh, they legalise gay marriage in 2017. So, you guys can have a proper wedding. I'll also have event planning experience by then, so I can organise it for you."

He frowns. "Is this some kind of sick joke?"

Kelsey looks taken aback. "Why would you say that?"

"Why are you making fun of me?"

"I'm not making fun of you! It's true!"

He shakes his head. "I've had enough of this 'game' now. Do you actually want to order something?"

"I'm so sorry about Kelsey," I say. "She was just trying to be nice."

"Well, I'd appreciate if you left my sexuality out of it, thanks. You have no idea how hard it is to live in a small coastal town where everyone is homophobic. And to make frivolous statements about how I'll apparently have to wait twenty years until I can finally marry someone I love is just hurtful."

Kelsey looks stricken. "Jackson! That wasn't my intention at all. I'm so sorry. You're one of my favourite people in the whole world. I would never want to upset you."

"How can I be one of your favourite people when we barely even know each other?"

It's true that back in 1997, we only knew Jackson because he worked at Beans. My relationship with him was mostly surface level until we reconnected after I broke up with Ed. And Kelsey was the same. She only became friends with him properly after she started coming to Brisbane to see me, and we'd all go out together.

"I know you better than you think. But I'll stop now, so I don't dig myself deeper into a hole. We'll have two double-shot espressos, please."

Kelsey shares my love of caffeine, although I still haven't tried to order something that strong in my teenage body.

"Actually, just a hot chocolate for me," I say.

Kelsey gives me an incredulous look. "Hot chocolate?"

"Yes, please," I say, trying to remind her with my eyes that she needs to start acting a little less conspicuously.

She sighs. "Okay. I'll have one, too. And we'll have them to go."

He smiles tightly. "Sure."

I hand over some money, trying to show how apologetic I am by reaching out with my other hand and stroking Jackson's arm. His eyes reflect his appreciation of my gesture.

After we've collected our drinks, we walk back out to the street.

"Please don't do anything like that again," I say.

"Fine. I was just trying to have a bit of fun. What's the point in getting to revisit the past if you can't use the knowledge?"

"There *is* no point in that regard. The only benefit is that you may obtain new information that can affect your perspective of the future. Like how I found out about Ed and Maddie."

Kelsey sips her drink and pulls a face. "I should have gone for the caffeine. Anyway, it sounds to me like visiting the past only brings heartache."

"That's not completely true. I mean, I met Kurt…"

"Oh, that's right. Wait. Let's go sit on the beach and you can fill me in on this mystery man."

The sky is a little overcast, but it's still a beautifully warm summer morning, and the ocean is calm and flat.

We sit under a palm tree on the grass behind the boardwalk, and Kelsey spends a moment taking it all in. It's strange, but to me, this feels just as normal as reality now.

"All right, so who is this Kurt?"

"I met him on my first trip back here. I was down at The Palace with Mum, and I went to the old record store across the road. He was working that day, and then I kept running into him randomly each time I came back."

"And?"

"And…I…"

"Oh my God! You're in love with a guy from the nineties, aren't you?" I blush. "Stop."

"Have you looked him up in the future?"

"Um, no. I sort of tried, but I didn't know his last name until yesterday. And there's something else…"

"What?"

"He's Rachel's cousin."

She squeals. "So why didn't you ask...." Her face dawns with recognition. "You *did* ask her, didn't you? That first night you reconnected. And she said he was living in London."

"Wow. I'm surprised you remember all that, considering how drunk we were."

"Actually, I can't remember anything else she said. What *did* she say?"

"That he had a model girlfriend."

"Oh, that's right. And you haven't asked for an update since?"

"No. But now that I know his last name is Hamilton, I can stalk him when we wake up."

"That's so trippy. Can you imagine? But what if he's not what you expected?"

"I guess at least then I can move on. But I need to anyway, since he has a girlfriend."

"That was last year! Things change."

"Yeah, he could be married now," I say gloomily.

"Do you want to go visit him today? Introduce me?"

I laugh. "We don't have to do that."

"But I'd like to."

"Are you sure? He won't know who I am."

"What else are we going to do with the day? Maybe he'll have a hot friend he can introduce me to."

"Actually, he used to occasionally hang out with Aaron."

"No way."

"Yeah, because of Rachel's brother, Chris. You remember how they were friends?"

"Oh, yeah. Well, it might be fun to see my future husband before he decided he liked me."

"Really?"

"Why not? What's the worst that could happen?"

"Um, have you already forgotten the incident with Jackson just now?"

"It's a good thing these are standalone realities then, isn't it?"

I roll my eyes. "I guess it is."

THIRTEEN

Kelsey and I catch the bus down to Maroochydore and get out near The Palace.

"I don't think Kurt's working today," I explain to her. "But I do know both his home and mobile number."

"Of course you do," she laughs. "And naturally, you would know his work schedule, too."

"What do you think I should say when I call?"

"I don't know. I would have thought you'd have all your plans and explanations worked out by now. How many times have you been back here anyway?"

"Um, four last year, and then one before I told you. So, this will be the seventh."

"And how many times have you run into Kurt?"

"All of them. Except, of course nothing happened between us until after Ed and I split up."

"Hmm…"

"I'm serious. I could tell he was interested before that, but I was never going to cheat on Ed."

"Well, if I meet a hot guy today who wants to kiss me, I'm certainly not going to be worried about Ben being upset."

"That's your decision."

"You think it's wrong?"

"I'm just saying, I felt an obligation to do the right thing by my husband. Just because he was never going to find out and I could possibly excuse my behaviour as being part of a dream, I still couldn't do it."

"Okay, okay. I get your point. But Ben and I aren't serious anyway."

"Then it's a non-issue."

I get out my mobile phone and dial Kurt's home number. He answers right away.

"Hello?"

My face breaks out into a big smile. "Hi, Kurt? I was just wondering, is Chris with you?"

"Uh, no. Who's asking?"

"Oh, sorry, it's Rachel's friend, Anna. She was asking me to pass on a message."

"Ah. Well, he didn't mention visiting today, but sometimes he just drops by unannounced. What was the message?"

"She wanted to ask him to bring back some music for her party. I'm guessing maybe from you?"

"That sounds about right. Do you know which albums she wanted?"

"Maybe Beastie Boys and Soundgarden…stuff like that?"

"How soon does she need it?"

"Tonight?"

"Well, if someone can come here to pick it up, I guess I can spare a few albums for a few days. But tell Rachel she has to look after them."

"Of course. Um, she has to get everything ready this afternoon, so would it be okay if I came? Her other friend Kelsey is with me, too."

He sighs. "Sure. You know where I live?"

"Sorry, no."

"I'm on Duporth Avenue. The Aqua Apartments. Number three."

"Great. Thanks! See you soon!"

"Okay."

Kelsey looks at me, impressed. "You *do* have this thing down pat. Good thinking."

"It's scary how easy it is to lie these days. But also, I stole the music excuse from you. That's how you introduced yourself to him yesterday."

"I can't believe I already met him yesterday as a seventeen-year-old, but it never actually happened. Hey, you don't lie this much in the future, do you?"

"Of course not. Except for hiding the information I learn here when I'm using it in the future. Clearly, I couldn't tell Ed how I really knew about Maddie."

She thinks for a second. "Hang on. Did you only contact me last year because you met me back here?"

"Pretty much."

"Far out."

"I'd like to think we would have reconciled eventually anyway."

"I hope so."

We walk down the road to the Aqua Apartments. It's a small, old-fashioned block of six set just back from the river. This land will be worth a fortune in the future.

I nervously knock on the door at number three.

Kurt appears after a few seconds—and he looks amazing. His hair is hanging wild and loose, and he has on a pair of old torn denim jeans. I can't stop looking at his bare chest and that constellation tattoo.

Kelsey nudges me as if to say *good job*.

"Uh, hi. I'm Anna, and this is Kelsey."

He stands to the side. "Hey. Come in."

It feels strange, getting to learn more about Kurt incrementally each visit and knowing he has no idea. I can imagine this is how Adam Sandler's character must have felt in *50 First Dates*.

I look around at the interior. It's a typical boy house, with a worn leather couch along one wall, and a big TV resting on a black cabinet along the other. The place smells like incense, and Alice in Chains is playing from a large stereo in the corner.

"Would you two like a drink?"

"Beer, please," Kelsey pipes up.

"Nice try. But no. If you go to school with Rachel, you're not eighteen yet."

"Just a glass of water would be fine, thank you," I say.

Kurt finally looks at me properly. His gaze stays fixed for a moment longer than necessary. "No problem."

My stomach flutters. It can't be coincidence that every single time we run into each other, he seems to react the same way.

He goes over to the kitchen, which is piled high with dirty dishes, and gets two glasses out of a cupboard. He fills them up at the tap and hands one to me and the other to Kelsey, but he keeps his eyes on me the whole time.

"Have we met?" he asks.

Kelsey giggles. I give her a warning look.

"Not unless you count the record store."

"I feel like it's more than that. But never mind." He goes over to a bunch of plastic milk crates filled with records and CDs. "I'm assuming you don't want vinyl?"

"Uh, probably not." I don't remember Rachel having a record player.

"Do you have any specific requests?"

"Just whatever you think."

He picks up a handful of CDs and flicks through them. "Here's a

Beastie Boys album. And Soundgarden. Did you want Nine Inch Nails?"

"Yeah, that would be good. Maybe some Foo Fighters, too?"

"Um, okay, I think I have their album somewhere."

"Oh, I haven't listened to them in ages," Kelsey says. "One of my all-time favourite songs is *Everlong*."

Kurt frowns. "I don't think I know that one. Is it on a B-Side collection or something?"

I bump Kelsey with my shoulder and look at her with wide eyes. I can't believe she's so bad at this. The song she's talking about won't be released until later in the year.

"I think maybe you were thinking of a different band?" I say pointedly.

"Oh, right. Yeah, the…um…*Food* Fighters."

Kurt wrinkles his brow. "The *Food* Fighters? They sound like a parody group."

"Not many people know them," Kelsey says, waving a hand dismissively. "But they're pretty awesome."

"I'll take your word for it." He pulls out a few more CDs and hands them to me. "Will this be enough?"

"Yes, I think so. Thank you."

"This party is tonight?"

"Yup."

"At Chris and Rachel's?"

"That's right."

"Do you know if their parents are going to be home? If not, I might see if Chris wants me to drop by. That way, I could bring a few more albums and keep an eye on them."

"I'm sure it would be fine," Kelsey answers for me. "You don't have any hot friends you could bring along as well, do you?"

I think she's forgotten that there isn't actually a party.

He laughs. "I guess I could see who's not doing anything tonight. I might be able to bring a buddy or two."

"Please do."

Kurt looks at me. "So, you're definitely going to be there?"

"Uh, yes?"

"You don't sound so sure."

"We'll both be there," Kelsey assures him. "Do you just want to bring all the albums at the same time?"

"Sure. What time do you think you'll need to set up?"

"Um, maybe 6:30pm for a 7pm start?" she says.

"Cool. I'll see you there, then."

"Great. We'll let you get back to whatever it was you were doing," I say.

"Oh, I was just studying. Nothing major. But yeah, I should probably get back to it."

He walks us to the door. It feels weird pretending that we haven't already made out. I so badly want to hug him and kiss him, but I obviously don't.

When we get to the door, he reaches out and briefly places his hand on my arm. "It was great meeting you both."

"You, too. We'll see you tonight!"

"You will."

He watches us leave. I turn back to see if he's gone back inside, but he's still standing there watching us. He rubs a hand across his mouth as if embarrassed he was caught staring. I give him a little wave, and then Kelsey and I run off down the road.

"Oh my God. How did you not throw yourself at that man the second you met him? It's like he's obsessed with you—yet in his reality, this is the first time you've met?"

"I know! Every time, there's this crazy chemistry between us."

"At least you know you'll get to see him again tonight."

"There's just one small problem."

"Pfft. We can easily fix that. Let's go and see Rachel."

"You really want to do this?"

"Sure! What's the use of travelling back in time if you can't do the stuff you're unable to do as an adult? Besides, it will be a good way to see everyone again."

"You might be disappointed."

"I don't care. What else are we going to do? I mean, I know we could go completely wild and test the limits of this reality, but somehow I don't think you'd be up for that."

"You thought right."

"And if Lover Boy brings along a friend or two, at least they'll be a bit closer to our real age."

"True. But it's still a sixteen-year difference."

"Who cares? Ben is eleven years younger than me."

"Ah. Yeah, I forgot you already have some practice with the younger generation."

"That's right. So, let's go have something to eat and then find a bus back to Shell Beach!"

***

After catching the bus to my place, Kelsey waits outside while I quickly run upstairs and grab a bag with a few things in it. I hurry back down and beg Mum to let me borrow the car.

"Wait, wait. Hang on a second. I've barely seen you these holidays. Tell me what you've been up to."

"Oh, not much. Just listening to music and hanging around."

"Why don't you do that here?"

"Maybe we will tomorrow. We're going to Rachel's this afternoon, and then I'll probably stay at Kelsey's tonight."

"Hmm…okay. You have your phone with you?" she asks.

"I do."

"All right. Drive safe."

"Thanks, Mum!"

I grab the keys and head out the front. "All good. Let's go."

We drive over to Rachel's, figuring it will be easier to convince her to have a party face-to-face.

"Man, this is such a trip," Kelsey says as we pull up in her driveway.

I notice someone watering the lawn next door and smile. "When you see who Rachel's neighbour is, you'll think it's even more of a trip."

Kelsey looks over and gasps. "Mr. Green!" How did I not know he lived next door to Rachel?"

"Beats me. I'm surprised you never looked him up in the phone book."

"Well, I did have a crush on him, but I wasn't obsessed or anything." She jumps out of the car and bounds on over. I follow behind but stand back a little.

"Ms. Gillespie. What are you doing here?"

"Hi, Mr. Green! We're just here to see Rachel! I didn't know you lived here."

"I only moved in a few months ago."

"Are you enjoying your summer holidays?"

"I am, thank you."

He looks awkward, like he's not sure how much of his professional façade to let slip.

"You look great today," Kelsey says. "I like that colour on you."

I stifle a laugh. Joe Green is wearing a mustard-coloured vest. I know Kelsey had a thing for him back in the nineties, but surely she's joking now?

He looks flustered. "Ah, thank you." He turns back to the tap and switches it off. "I'll see you when term starts. Enjoy your last week and a half of freedom."

"Oh, we will." Kelsey gives him a huge smile as he hurries inside. He glances quickly at me and then disappears.

Kelsey comes back over. "Aw, the poor thing thought I was going to jump him."

"Does he live up to your teenage dreams?" I ask.

"You know what? I *do* understand what I saw in him. And he's a lot younger than I thought he was back then. Maybe only early thirties?"

"I guess anyone over twenty-five seemed ancient back then."

"Ha. Yeah."

We walk up to Rachel's front door, and I knock.

She opens the door. "Oh, hey, guys. What's up?"

"Can we come in for a bit? We have a proposition for you."

"Sounds intriguing. What kind of proposition?"

We head to Rachel's bedroom and sit on her queen-sized waterbed.

"I forgot you had this," Kelsey says, rocking around on it like a little kid.

"Yeah, okay." She rolls her eyes at Kelsey and then turns to me. "What do you need?"

"How do you feel about having a last-minute party tonight?"

"Is that all?"

"Yes. What do you think?"

"Um, I guess. Isn't it a bit late to get the word out, though?"

"I'm sure we'll manage. I don't mind making the phone calls, as long as it's cool with your parents."

"I don't think it will be a problem. I'll tell them to go out. They're always looking for an excuse to drink with their friends."

"And your cousin Kurt said he can bring the music."

She looks confused. "How do you know Kurt? And how come you were talking to him?"

"Chris introduced us the other day," Kelsey improvises.

"Oh. But that doesn't explain why you were talking to him today."

"We'll tell you everything in good time. So, it's a yes for the party?"

"Why the hurry?"

"I don't know. Why not?"

She shakes her head. "You guys are so weird. All right. You want to start organising now?"

"Yes!"

She gets out a notebook with all her phone numbers listed. "Okay. Who should we call first?"

FOURTEEN

"Do you think Mr. Green is hot?" Kelsey asks Rachel during a lull in planning. The older version of Rachel looks so different to this version that for now I can pretend she's not the same person I'm currently fighting with.

Rachel bursts out laughing. "Uh, no. Why? Do you?"

"Yeah, I do."

Lucky for Kelsey, she won't have to worry about the repercussions of admitting that out loud for very long.

"But he's so old!" Rachel says. "And boring. What do you think, Anna?"

"I'm not a huge fan," I agree.

"I can't believe you're admitting to liking a teacher!" Rachel says.

"What's the big deal?" Kelsey asks.

"I don't know. It's just strange."

"Whatever. And speaking of older guys, how come you never told us about your grunge-god cousin before?"

"Um, because he's my cousin, and I don't see him that way?"

"But surely you can tell he's good looking."

"I don't know. Why does it matter? Do you want me to hook you up with him?"

"Normally I wouldn't say no, but I'm pretty sure he only has eyes for

Anna."

"What? How? Did this just happen today? Start at the beginning."

I pretend to concentrate on an article in a magazine about throwing an epic summer party while Kelsey comes up with a story about how she had an appointment with a modelling agency and took me along for support. Apparently, afterwards, we'd passed the record store and gotten talking to Kurt.

"I can't believe he likes Anna! Anna, how do you feel about this?"

"Um, he's pretty cute," I say, embarrassed. I'm not used to talking about him with other people yet.

"Well, I guess that's kind of cool. So, is this why you want to have this last-minute party?"

"It's one reason. But do we really need an excuse?"

"I suppose not."

I'm excited that I get to see Kurt again, but after the last party I came to here at Rachel's house, I'm not eager for a repeat performance.

As if reading my mind, Rachel suddenly pipes up. "Oh, what about Todd? It might be awkward having him here if you're going to be with Kurt, but it wouldn't be fair to exclude him when all his friends are going to be invited."

"Just do whatever. I'll figure it out. I'm sure Todd won't care." In Todd's world, June last year would be an entire lifetime ago. I can't remember who he dated after me, but I'm sure he'd have moved on by now.

"Okay. And I assume you'll want Aaron here, Kelsey?"

"Oh, no! That's fine. You don't have to invite him."

"But he's friends with Chris. If Chris finds out we're having a party, I won't be able to stop him inviting him. And I thought you were obsessed with the guy."

"I'm having second thoughts. But you can ask him to come if you want."

"Have you gone off him?"

"You could say that."

"I only saw you both yesterday, but I feel like it's been way longer," Rachel muses. "You guys have whole different lives going on."

I shoot Kelsey a look. We have to start acting more naturally.

"I've always been like this," Kelsey says breezily. "Anna is just along for the ride. But I'm sorry, babe. I should have invited you too, today. I promise I will next time."

"Thanks."

"Can Chris get us alcohol?"

"Probably. Do you have any money?"

Kelsey opens her purse and hands over nearly all the cash she has. She then gets my purse and does the same. I still don't think Kelsey fully understands the implications for this reality if it continues beyond today.

"Any requests?" Rachel asks wryly.

"Uh, whatever Chris thinks. Hey, do you mind continuing with the phone calls while Anna takes me home to get some clothes?"

"You want to borrow some of mine?"

"Aw, that's sweet, but I'd feel more comfortable in my own stuff. We won't be long."

"Sure. Do you want to pick up some snacks on the way as well?"

"We can do that. We'll be back soon!"

Kelsey and I head out to the car and drive back to her place. Just as we're walking up to the front door, it flies open, and a young woman runs out with tears streaming down her face.

She pushes past us and keeps going. I notice that her shirt is torn.

"Hey!" Kelsey calls. "Are you okay?"

She doesn't answer and keeps going.

Kelsey and I look at each other and hurry inside.

Andy is sitting in front of the TV as if everything is completely normal.

"Who was that?" Kelsey demands.

"Who was who?" he asks, playing dumb.

"The girl who just ran out of here crying?"

"Oh, you mean Samantha," he says vaguely, not taking his eyes off the TV.

"What was wrong with her?"

"I don't know."

Kelsey stomps over to the TV and switches it off. "What did you do to her?"

He looks up, surprised. "I didn't do anything. And why do you care?"

"Did you rape her?"

He laughs. "Are you fucking serious?"

"Yes, I am."

He picks up the remote and turns the TV back on. "No."

"Okay, then," Kelsey says casually and heads for the stairs. I follow. Under her breath she says, "You won't mind me checking your bedroom for evidence, then, will you?"

"Kelsey, do you think this is a good idea?" I whisper.

"I can't stand back and do nothing."

"But it won't make any difference. You know that."

"It will make a difference today." She enters Andy's room and starts rummaging through his drawers. "Come and help me look for where he hides his drugs. What does Rohypnol look like?"

"I have no idea. Kelsey, what if Andy gets violent?"

"Just...a...second..." She opens a drawer containing winter clothes and feels around in the back. "Aha!" She pulls out a small wooden box and opens it before lifting out a plastic bag filled with small white round tablets. "I don't think this is Advil," she says.

"What are you going to do with them?" I ask, nervously looking down the stairs for signs of Andy coming up.

"What I should have done when I suspected him of being up to no good the first time around. I mean, I never actually looked for proof, but I had a feeling he was doing something bad long before he was caught." She pulls me into her room and locks the door. "Give me your phone."

"Why?"

"I'm calling the police."

"Are you sure?"

"Yep." I notice her eyes are starting to tear up. "I know it's not going to affect the future, but I have to do it anyway."

"Okay." I hand over my mobile and watch as Kelsey dials the local station.

"Hi. Um, I want to report a possible crime. I found a bag of pills in my brother's bedroom, and I think they may be Rohypnol. Also, a girl just ran out of our house crying. I worry he might have done something to her, and that he might do it again soon."

She listens for a moment. "Yes, he's here now."

Another beat and then she says her address. She hangs up and looks at me grimly. "They're sending someone over."

"What do you want to do?"

"I guess wait until they arrive." Her face falls. "I'm not sure I feel like going to a party now. But you can still go."

"I'm not leaving you on your own."

"I won't mind."

"I will."

We sit in silence for what seems like forever. And then we hear voices downstairs. Andy sounds defiant at first, but his tone soon turns nasty.

Kelsey unlocks her bedroom door and tiptoes across the landing to the top of the stairs. I have no idea what to do. I haven't yet been in a potentially violent situation during one of these visits.

"You don't have a fucking thing on me," he snarls.

"We've had a report that you are in possession of a controlled substance and may have also assaulted a female."

"Did my sister tell you that? Kelsey? Get the fuck down here!"

"Is anyone else here?" a voice calls up.

"Uh, I'm here with a friend of mine," Kelsey says nervously.

"Would you both mind coming down here, please?"

Kelsey motions to me, and I reluctantly follow her. Two police officers are standing in the living room. Andy is standing between them. When we both reach the bottom of the stairs, Andy tries to lunge towards Kelsey, but the police officers restrain him.

"I found these," Kelsey says, holding out the bag.

Andy's eyes widen. "Where did you get those?"

"In your bottom drawer."

"Bitch." He tries to struggle out of the police officers' grasp again, but they hold him tight.

"I think you'd better come with us down to the station," one of them says.

"I'm not fucking going anywhere."

"Then I'm afraid we'll have to place you under arrest."

"I can't believe you would do this to your own fucking brother," Andy spits at Kelsey.

"I can't believe you drug women and rape them," she snaps back.

"Easy there," one of the police officers says. "We'll get to the bottom of this. Kelsey, is it? Do you mind coming down to the station, too? And your friend?"

"Sure. Is that okay, Anna?"

I'm a little shell-shocked from the whole incident and don't say anything for a moment. I'm guessing this is some sort of catharsis for her. Maybe she felt a lot of guilt over what happened the first time around and needs to treat this like a proper do-over.

"Yeah, okay."

Andy struggles a little more, but the officers manage to get him outside and into their car. Kelsey waits until they have him secure before handing over the bag of pills.

"Thank you. We'll see you in a few minutes."

Kelsey and I get back in the car.

"Do you want to let Rachel know we're no longer coming to the party we begged her to have?" I ask.

"Yeah, I guess so. Shit. I haven't done this day very well, have I?"

"It could have gone a little smoother," I admit.

"It's just...I don't know...it was like this force came over me, and I absolutely had to do something. Like the universe would know if I turned a blind eye for a second time."

"Remember, it's not your fault," I say gently. "You were only a teenager. Who knows what Andy would have done to you if he felt threatened?"

"But who knows how many women's lives he ruined as a result of me being a coward?"

"You're not a coward."

"I am."

We drive down the road in silence. Kelsey stares out her side window.

"Wait! Stop!"

"What?" I slam on the brakes.

"It's that girl! Samantha! In the park there."

I pull over onto the side of the road and look where Kelsey is pointing. She's right. Samantha is sitting on a park bench, crying her eyes out.

Kelsey jumps out of the car and runs over to her. I follow close behind.

Samantha looks up, afraid as we get near her.

"Leave me alone," she moans.

"We just wanted to check on you," Kelsey says. "I called the police and they arrested Andy."

Her eyes widen. "Really?"

"Yes. We're on our way to the station to answer some questions. I found Rohypnol in his bedroom, so I gave it to the cops as well."

She shakes her head. "Wow."

"Is your name Samantha?" Kelsey asks.

She frowns. "No. It's Melanie."

Yikes. I shouldn't have expected Andy to tell the truth, but the way he lied so seamlessly before makes my blood run cold.

Kelsey seems to be thinking the same thing, but quickly recovers.

"Melanie, I want to say how sorry I am for whatever my brother did. I'm going to do everything I can to make sure he's punished for it."

"I think I want to go home now."

"You can come with us to the station? We'll back you up."

"No. I don't think I could handle talking about everything and having the cops wonder if I'm telling the truth or not."

"We know you're telling the truth."

"I can't. Sorry."

"Then can we take you home? Or to a friend's house? You shouldn't be alone, particularly if you've got Rohypnol in your system."

"I have a friend who lives nearby. I can walk there."

"We'll go with you."

"No! Please. Just leave me alone." She stands up, looking unsteady on her feet. I instinctively reach out to prevent her from falling, but she recoils from my touch. I lower my hands.

I get out my phone. "Here. Call your friend on my phone and we'll wait with you until they arrive. We can't leave you by yourself like this."

She reluctantly takes the handset and dials a number. "Hi, Beck? Yeah, I'm just in the park behind your place and I feel a little weird. Do you mind coming down and meeting me?"

She listens for a second. "Thanks." After she hangs up, she says, "She'll be here in a minute."

"Good. And I'd maybe consider going to the doctor as well," Kelsey suggests.

"I just want to forget what happened," she says.

"Can I at least get your number or something? I can call you and give you an update on Andy."

She hesitates for a second. "Okay."

Kelsey rummages around in her bag for a pen and scrap of paper. "Melanie...sorry, what was your last name?"

"Arthur."

"Here, can you write down your number for me?"

Melanie shakily takes the pen and scrawls her number on the paper.

"Don't let Andy get hold of this."

"I promise I won't."

We sit with her until a stocky brunette comes over to meet us. She eyes Melanie worriedly. "Are you okay, hon?"

"I, um, think maybe I have food poisoning or something. Do you mind if I hang at your place for a bit?"

"Sure." She looks at us questioningly.

"Oh, we have to go. We just noticed Melanie didn't look well and wanted to stay with her until you arrived," I explain.

"Thank you," she says gratefully.

We leave them to it and get back in the car.

"Are you going to look her up in the real world?" I ask.

"I don't know yet. But I'd like to see if she turned out okay."

"You know what happened to me when I decided to track someone down in the future?"

"I know. But ever since I found out what Andy did, I've really struggled with my part in the whole thing."

"You are not to blame for this. And if you do track Melanie down, tread carefully."

"I will."

We reach the station. Just before we get out of the car, I hold up my phone. "We still need to call Rachel. Do you want to call her and break the bad news, or should I?"

"I'll do it. Man, I'll be glad when this twelve hours is up."

You and me both, I think wryly.

FIFTEEN

Kelsey and I spend the rest of the afternoon talking to a police officer about what we know. I think Kelsey is telling them things she learned in the future after Andy got arrested then, to ensure they properly investigate him now. She also gives them Melanie's name so they can call her to corroborate her story. I'm not sure how appreciative Melanie will be about that.

We're finally released just after 7pm, and Kelsey and I wearily leave the station. Thankfully, the police are going to hold onto Andy for a bit longer.

"What do you want to do now?" I ask.

"I don't know. But I definitely don't feel like going to a party. How much longer until we wake up?"

"Well, technically, you won't wake up until the morning, but you'll pass out here in about an hour and a half."

"I seriously don't know how you've been able to do this six times already. It's such a mind-fuck."

"Well, yeah. But the first couple of times were a novelty. And the last time I came back last year was because I wanted to see you without having to go through an emotional reconciliation."

"Oh, babe." She wraps me in a hug. "Life is way more complicated than we think, huh?"

"Yup. So, what did Rachel say when you called her earlier?"

"She was surprisingly good about it. I told her we'd try and come if we had time later, but there was a chance we wouldn't make it."

"Do you think maybe we could go for the last half hour we're in 1997? Just so I can say goodbye to Kurt?"

"Oh, of course. I just don't think I could handle the idea of going to a teen party right now. I mean, with Aaron there…"

"I totally understand. So, what would you like to do for the next hour?"

"I don't know. I don't want to go home, and I don't know about your place, either. Where's somewhere quiet we can have something to eat and chill out?"

I think for a second. "I have an idea."

***

I decide to drive Kelsey out to the lookout Kurt and I visited recently. We stop at a Pizza Hut on the way and pick up a supreme pizza. "Oh, I miss the proper Pizza Hut dine-in restaurants," Kelsey says, looking around. "Hey, haven't they resurrected some of these recently?"

"Yeah, I think I heard that."

"Remind me to find out where they are when we get back."

"Ha. Okay."

We wait for our pizza to be ready and then continue on to the lookout.

I park the car, and we sit on a nearby bench, the town of Shell Beach twinkling below us.

Kelsey helps herself to a slice of pizza and eats it, her eyes glazed over.

"Do you want to talk about anything?" I ask.

"Not really. I just feel numb. And a bit sick. I kind of wish this was the actual past, so I could make a real difference."

"You can't live your life with regrets. And like I said before, none of this was your fault. It was all Andy. And surely your mum should have realised something was happening. Why didn't she do anything?"

"Because Mum lives in her own fucking bubble world," she says bitterly.

"Do you think she struggled after your dad left?"

"I don't know. Probably. I mean, I know what it's like to go through a marriage breakup, and how hard it is to move on afterwards, but she should have gotten over it and looked after us. That was her job! I never felt like I had an adult who cared about me." She starts crying.

I pull her head over to rest on my shoulder. "Sweetie, I'm sure that's not true. What about relatives? And the teachers at school? I'm sure they all cared about your wellbeing."

"Never on a level that mattered."

"You still turned out okay. I always thought you were a pretty cool chick."

"Yeah, but we went for so long without talking! And I was too scared to make that first move to call you again. I've had so much rejection in my life that I couldn't bear it again with you."

"Oh, Kels. I'm sorry I didn't contact you sooner. I promise no matter what happens in the future, we'll always work it out, and I'll never abandon you again, okay?"

She sniffs. "Okay."

"Why don't we just forget about all the crap for now and eat this awesomely greasy pizza and enjoy the view of this town before the hipsters took over?"

She chokes out a laugh. "Sounds good."

***

Just before eight, we head back over to Rachel's. "Are you okay with this?" I check.

"Yeah, it's fine. I think I can cope with half an hour of nostalgia."

"Thank you. I appreciate it."

"I'm happy to be your wing woman, no matter the year."

I laugh. "The sign of a true friend."

We pull up outside Rachel's house and see the driveway full of party revellers. It's not unlike the party I revisited last year.

"Whoa. This is seriously weird," Kelsey says.

"I know. Try going back to the exact same party as the first time around. That's even weirder."

We get out of the car and make our way up to the house. A few people give us a nod of acknowledgement. We find Rachel in the living room, talking to her brother Chris. Who is also with Aaron.

"Wow," Kelsey whispers. "Why was I so obsessed with that guy? He looks like such a douchebag, even here."

"I guess your tastes change as you mature," I whisper back.

"Hey, Rachel," I say, going up to them. "We are so sorry about everything…asking you to hold a last-minute party and then not even being able to show up."

"It's okay. You're here now, and the night is still young." She turns to Kelsey. "Are you all right? What happened with Andy?"

"Long story. I'll tell you about it another time."

I glance at Aaron. He's watching Kelsey with a mixture of wariness and confusion. I guess he's used to her throwing herself at him all the time, but she's completely ignoring him now.

A Beastie Boys song comes on, and I look over at the stereo. He's here. He looks up at the exact same moment, and our eyes connect. His face breaks out into a big grin.

I shyly walk over. "Hey."

"Hey! Rachel said you might not make it. But you're here!"

"Yeah, there was a bit of drama with Kelsey's brother. But it's all sorted now."

"I'm so glad you could come. Hang out with me while I figure out a playlist for the rest of the evening."

"Sure." I sit down on the floor beside him and look at the CDs he brought along. "Thanks so much for bringing the entertainment."

"It was my pleasure. Can I confess something?"

"If you like."

"The only reason I'm here is because I wanted to see you again."

"Is that so?" I say teasingly. "I hoped that was the case."

He beams. "Any requests? What's your favourite song?"

I try to remember what my actual favourite song was back in 1997.

"*Glory Box* by Portishead."

"Ooh, nice choice." He finds a CD in his crate and gets it ready to put on once the current song is finished.

"What about you?" I ask. "What's yours?"

He thinks for a minute. "*Plush* by Stone Temple Pilots."

"I heard that the lyrics for that song are a metaphor for a lost obsessive relationship."

He looks at me intently. "Is that right? I never thought to find out what it meant. I normally like to decide my own meaning."

"I know what you mean. Like *Closer* by Nine Inch Nails. Its lyrics are kind of depressing, but the song is pretty sexy anyway."

He laughs. "Very sexy."

I blush. I feel like he's not just talking about the song.

"Oh, actually, there is one other song I discovered recently that I love, but you might not have heard of it."

"What's it called?"

"*Darkness*, by Larkin."

My eyes widen. "That's…"

At that moment, something wet splashes over the two of us. I look up in shock and see Todd hovering above us.

"Oops," he says, holding an empty glass.

"What the hell, man?" Kurt says, standing up and shaking himself off.

"I tripped," Todd says. "Sorry."

"Apologise to Anna."

"Um, no. I don't think so."

"Apologise now."

Todd starts to walk away. "See ya."

Kurt grabs his shirt and pulls him back. "You're not leaving until you say sorry."

I sit there, frozen, ignoring the cold liquid seeping through my top.

Todd tries to swing at Kurt, but he deflects. "I think it's time for you to leave, buddy." He raises an eyebrow at Chris, who comes over.

"What's the problem?" he asks.

"This guy has outstayed his welcome."

"Okay, then."

Chris grabs one of Todd's arms and Kurt keeps hold of the other as they wrestle him out the door.

Kelsey only just seems to notice what's happening and comes hurrying over.

"Oh my God. What was that all about?"

"I guess Todd doesn't like seeing me talk to anyone else."

"Weird." She leans in and smells me. "What did he throw on you?"

"I'm guessing rum and Coke."

"Ugh. Maybe you should ask Rachel if you can borrow a clean top."

"Does it really matter?" I look at the clock on the wall. "We have about ten minutes left."

"Shit. Already? What do we do?"

"Just act normal. Or maybe find a couch if you don't want to hit your head on the ground."

"This is so bizarre."

"You kind of get used to it."

"I don't think I *want* to get used to it."

Kurt reappears. "Hey, are you all right?"

"I'm fine. Thanks for looking out for me. Are *you* all right?"

"Yeah, I've dealt with worse." He looks at my top and then his own and grabs my hand. "Let's go clean up. I'm sure my cousins can spare a change of clothes."

I've suddenly changed my mind about it being worthwhile.

"Be back in a sec," I say to Kelsey, with a cheeky smile.

She winks. "Okay."

Kurt pulls me into what I'm assuming is Chris's bedroom. I sit on the edge of the bed while he opens the wardrobe and starts rummaging around in a drawer. He pulls out a plain black t-shirt. "I guess this will do for me. Sorry, we should have looked in Rachel's room for you first." He pulls his shirt off over his head and hangs it over a chair.

"I don't mind," I say. I can't help myself. I stand up and trace my fingers over his tattoo. I'm fascinated by it.

"I've wanted to do this all day," I murmur.

He chuckles. "I've wanted to do *this* all day." He lifts my chin with his hand and leans down to press his lips on mine. I sigh with happiness and pull him closer. And then I realise I'm still covered in rum and Coke. I step back for a second to lift my shirt over my head.

Kurt clears his throat, and his pupils dilate. He pulls me in again and kisses the top of my head.

"Holy shit, Anna. Where did you come from?"

I press my cheek to his chest. I almost tell him the truth but laugh quietly instead.

The room starts spinning, and I hold onto Kurt for support.

"Thank you for everything," I whisper as the room starts to fade.

"I don't know what you're thanking me for, but either way, it's my pleasure," he says.

And then everything goes black.

SIXTEEN

Kelsey and I wake up, back in my apartment. I open my eyes first, but Kelsey is only a few seconds behind.

I sit up and watch as she returns to reality. She stares at me, and then bursts out laughing. "Oh my God!"

"What a trip, huh?"

"You can say that again."

She sits up and looks down at her body. "That shit was insane."

"I know."

She looks at her watch. "I swear it felt like we just passed out, but it's the morning?"

"Yep."

"How did you cope the first time you went through that?"

"I don't know. I thought it was a dream, I guess. The second time around, I figured out a bit more, like the fact that the future wasn't affected, and that each day stood on its own."

"So, you thought maybe you were in a *Back to the Future* situation that first day?"

"I did."

"That would have been scary." She jumps up. "I need a shower. And some breakfast. I don't feel like anything is real anymore."

"I know what you mean."

She stops for a second. "Melanie."

"There's no hurry to look her up," I say gently.

"I know, but I want to see if she's okay." She picks up her phone and opens an internet browser.

"She might not welcome the reminder over twenty years later," I warn.

"I'm pretty sure she wouldn't need reminding."

"That's not what I meant, but as Andy's sister, you might do more harm than good."

After a moment, Kelsey nods as if satisfied. "I found her. She's a psychiatrist who specialises in domestic violence."

"That's interesting."

"I feel like she might be okay with me contacting her, but I won't rush into it. I have too much of my own stuff to process first."

I watch as she heads to the bathroom. I know exactly how she's feeling right now. It's so hard to reconcile the two realities.

I think about Kurt, and my heart aches. I hurry over to my laptop and switch it on. I open Google and type in *Kurt Hamilton music producer*.

There he is.

The air goes out of my lungs as I sit there staring at a photo of Kurt in the real world. In actual reality.

His hair is shorter, cut just above his shoulders, but he is still sexy as hell. I wouldn't have thought it possible, but I'm even more attracted to him now.

His photo links to a news article on a music website. I leave it for the moment and look at what else I can find on him. He doesn't have his own website or any social media apart from a Twitter account, and even that only has half a dozen generic posts I'm pretty sure were done by someone else.

I go back to the article and read it. It was written in June last year and features Kurt in a Top 10 list of influential music producers in the industry. He sits at number six.

"I was heavily influenced by the Australian dance scene in the mid to late nineties," says Kurt Hamilton, the genius behind DJs Grant, Dizzy and March Fly. *"I remember listening to Larkin's* Darkness *in 1997 and thinking it was the most amazing thing I'd ever heard."*

Oh my God! That song! He mentioned that song again! But how can that be when it was a different timeline? Was he bound to discover it anyway?

"Of course, this was also the grunge era, so I basically lived on a diet of Smashing Pumpkins and Stone Temple Pilots. But it was the dance stuff that stayed with me decades later."

However, Hamilton is quick to point out he appreciates everything from Bob Dylan to Shaggy—the latter he admits to with a sheepish smile. "Hey, Boombastic *is a catchy tune. I'm not a music snob."*

Indeed, this shows in the diverse range of tracks he has produced, resulting in an impressive number of Grammy awards for his acts.

A notoriously private person, little is known about the man nicknamed Goldfinger—an affectionate term bestowed on someone whose every project has become a huge commercial success. But if the rumours are true, Kurt is happily settled, and possibly on the verge of marrying Norwegian model Olivia Pedersen.

I stop reading there. I don't want to think about Kurt marrying someone else. Especially a Norwegian model. I'm still sitting there, staring at his photo when Kelsey comes back, freshly washed and chewing on a protein bar she must have found in my cupboard.

She peers over my shoulder.

"Wow. You certainly know how to pick 'em." She skims the article. "Hey, we loved that Larkin song too, huh? Funny. It's a shame he's in London. I wonder who this Olivia is?"

"I don't think I want to know."

She nudges me out of the way and types on my keyboard before covering her mouth.

"Look!"

She points to an image of a woman I assume is Olivia. And she looks surprisingly like me. If I was tall and an actual model.

"Um, that's not depressing at all," I say.

"But it proves you'd be his type."

"Not really. It proves he likes models."

"We need to find out more. Like how serious they are. If, in fact, they're even still together."

"Stop," I say, feeling uneasy. "I can't do this. I don't want to know more. It will just make me depressed if I find out they're engaged or something."

"But they might also not be doing so well. Don't you think it's better to know either way?"

"No. He's still in London. Besides, I can always go back and see him in 1997."

"But for how long? You said you only have a limited number of Youth Compound doses left. And then what?"

"Then I'll deal with however I'm feeling at the time."

Kelsey shakes her head. "Okay, fine." She can see any further arguing will just make me resist more. "I guess we should try and enjoy our last weekend of freedom. Have you got all your RSVPs for next Saturday?"

"Yep. Everyone's coming."

"Great. I just have to confirm a few of my guests this week. I'm guessing Rachel is one of mine now?"

"Yeah, if you don't mind."

"You'll have to talk to her eventually."

"I did yesterday, remember?"

"You know I mean the grown-up version of her. Anyway, I'm going to head home. I'll see you on Monday at the café. Call me if you need anything beforehand."

"Will do."

"And Anna?"

"Yeah?"

"Maybe hold off on going back to 1997 until after we open. I just think it will be too much of a distraction. We need to concentrate on getting this thing right, and I can't afford to have you absent for a whole day this week."

"Okay."

She gives me a quick hug and heads for the door. "Bye!"

"Bye."

I feel angsty the whole rest of Saturday. By Sunday, I am dying to take the compound again. It is really the only day I can take it now for a couple of weeks. Next weekend is going to be busy, and then we open the following Tuesday. After that, Kelsey and I have decided to have Mondays and Tuesdays off, since we anticipate the weekends will be busy. That means I'll have to wait fifteen days at a minimum before I can see Kurt again.

I don't like the idea of that at all.

But I did agree to Kelsey that I'd hold off. I'm strong. I can do this.

***

I manage to get through the rest of Sunday by binge-watching several seasons of *Younger*. I can totally relate to Liza, pretending to be younger than she really is. I'd like to see her fake being a sixteen-year-old, though. The only downside of the show is when I see Josh on screen, his hair reminds me of Rachel's friend, Billy. Ugh.

And then my mind loops back to that kiss with the other mystery guy. I still can't believe I did that! It was almost like I was drugged or something. Well, majorly drunk, I guess. I'm so glad I left early. It would have been embarrassing having to deal with him in the real world afterwards.

The beginning of the week rolls around, and Kelsey and I are busy at the café. Monday and Tuesday are spent putting all our plates, cutlery, and glassware into their respective places. On Wednesday, we invite our new staff in for some training and a casual get-together. I've made up some petits fours for everyone to eat.

I let Kelsey lead the meeting. My brain is still firmly stuck in 1997 and those last few moments with Kurt. I want him so badly, I can barely think straight.

"Okay, so we've done up the rosters for the first month," Kelsey explains. "We've tried to accommodate any personal preferences, so Xander, I have you on early shifts each day, and Jax, the afternoon. Emery, you'll be the middle of the day and overlap with the other two. Sound good?"

They nod.

"Anna? Any info you need to pass on to your staff?"

I blink. I was just remembering the time I massaged sunscreen into Kurt's smooth chest at Shell Beach.

"Oh, um, no. I think we're good here."

She gives me a weird look but doesn't say anything. She turns back to the others. "All right, then…"

My phone starts ringing. It's Ed. I wonder what he wants. I stand up and head for the front door. "I'll be back in a second," I call out to everyone.

I click the *Answer* key. "Hello? Ed?"

"Hi, it's Maddie."

"Oh. Hi. Is everything okay? Why are you calling from Ed's phone?"

"Um, yeah, so Ed is here, too. We thought it would be best to tell you this together."

"Tell me what?" A heavy feeling sits in my chest.

"We're having a baby."

I feel as if the ground has dropped out from under me. I collapse against the nearest wall, leaning my face on the rough concrete rendering. I drop the phone to my side, but don't let go of it.

"Anna? Are you there?" Maddie's voice sounds far away.

I look down at the handset and click the *End Call* button.

I stay leaning on the wall for a few minutes. Nobody walking by seems to think it's strange, and no one inside comes to check on me.

I can't handle this. I look at the time. It's 4pm. I need to get away.

I'm going home and using that damn compound.

And I'm going to sleep with Kurt.

SEVENTEEN

I catch a cab home, texting Kelsey to let her know something came up, and switch off my phone. As soon as I'm inside my apartment, I race to the kitchen, grab a glass of water and mix up the compound. I gulp it down and throw myself on the couch. I don't even care if I get a crick in my neck from sleeping out here.

Huh.

I was in such a hurry to go back to 1997, that I forgot to check in my diary and see what I did on this day.

I wake up on a plane.

What on earth?

My sister is sitting next to me, listening to a Walkman, and flicking through a magazine. I look around and notice my parents sitting next to us on the other side of the aisle.

I have headphones over my ears, and Alanis Morissette's *You Oughta Know* is playing.

Where are we going? Are we flying away from home or back? I quickly shuffle through the pocket in front of me and find my boarding pass.

Okay. We're heading home from Sydney.

That's sort of a relief.

But what time will we get back? Even in the most optimistic scenario, if we land in less than half an hour, it's still going to be another hour after that before we get home. That will make it around six-thirty at the earliest—and then I'll somehow have to get down to Maroochydore to see Kurt...

I worry that I won't be able to pull this off.

I fidget restlessly in my seat. This is even worse than being back in the future. I can't physically move. And this was in the days before iPads and TVs on the back of your seat. I have nothing apart from this Walkman to distract me.

I look towards the front of the plane and see a couple of attendants with a food cart slowly making their way towards us. Great. That means we're not even halfway through the flight.

I jump up and make my way down to the back of the plane and lock myself in the toilet. I splash water on my face and pat it dry with a scratchy paper towel.

I stare at myself in the mirror. The novelty of looking at teenage me has worn off. All I can see is the distress of someone who has just been given extremely crappy news.

Ed is having a baby with Maddie.

Ed! The guy who took six years to propose and then said he never wanted kids is now having one with a woman he's only been back in touch with for seven months. It just seems unfair! What was so wrong with me that he couldn't bear the idea of us starting a family together?

Does this mean they're going to get married, too? He's already taken on half her mortgage and is living in her house. Why not make it the full trifecta?

It sucks that I basically instigated all of this. And what do I have in return? A pretend relationship with a guy who is sixteen years younger than me and has time-travel-induced amnesia.

I'm still going to sleep with him, though.

I pull open the door and find myself jammed in the service area while the flight attendants serve in the middle of the aisle. I jump from foot to foot. I guess it's better than being strapped into a seat.

A few minutes later, I finally get an opportunity to get around the serving cart. An unappetising-looking meal is waiting on my tray-table. I move it so I can sit back down and examine the contents. A stale bread roll, some anaemic fruit salad, and a foil-covered container, that when opened reveals a runny brown curry and some overcooked rice.

I wasn't hungry before, but I'm certainly not now.

Amy seems to be ravenous though, and ends up eating all her food, as well as most of mine. I don't even have the luxury of looking out the window, because I'm in an aisle seat. I stare straight ahead and pray that we begin our descent soon.

***

An hour later, we finally land. It feels like every step of the disembarking process, including baggage collection, is moving in super-slow-mo.

While we're standing at the luggage carousel, I sidle up to Mum.

"Would it be okay if I went to see Kelsey tonight?"

Mum rolls her eyes. "We've only been away for a couple of days. Can't you wait until tomorrow?"

"But I need to talk to her about something!"

"What's so important that you need to tell her in person and not over the phone?"

"It's…it's kind of private."

"No deal. If it's serious, you need to tell me, and I'll come to my own conclusions."

I flounder around for a suitable excuse. I can't come up with anything apart from the dumb story I used on myself once before.

I lower my voice. "She thinks she might be pregnant. I want to go and see if she's okay. If I call, her mum might accidentally pick up the other phone, and she doesn't want her to know until she's figured out what to do."

Mum looks horrified. Granted, not as horrified as when I said the same thing, but still. "She needs to tell her mother!"

"She will. But not yet. So, can I go, please?"

"Who's the father?"

"Some guy from school," I improvise.

"Oh, the poor things. That's going to make their lives so difficult."

"She called me yesterday and told me. I think she'd appreciate if I stayed over at her place tonight. And then I promise I'll stay home for the rest of the school holidays."

Mum still looks a little shell-shocked. I feel bad for inflicting this situation on her twice, but to make myself feel better, I'm going to pretend this particular universe does not continue on after I leave.

"Okay. Just this once. And I'd like you to stick to that promise about spending a bit more time at home. We've hardly seen you all summer, and even the last couple of days, it's like you've been in another world."

I almost laugh out loud. If only she knew.

"Thanks, Mum."

"And just remember, you're working an early shift tomorrow, so make sure you get some sleep tonight."

At least I'll be gone by 5am and won't have to worry about that.

"I will."

We catch a cab home, me looking at my watch the whole time. It's already late.

As soon as we get in the door, I run up to my room and dig out my phone. I call Kelsey, but she doesn't answer, so I leave a message to say I'm using her as an excuse and I'll fill her in tomorrow (not going to happen) and then I dial Kurt's home number. It rings out. I try his mobile, but it's switched off. Damn.

I call Rachel, and she answers right away. "Hello?"

"Oh, hey, it's Anna."

"You're back!"

"Uh, yeah, we just got home. Hey, you don't happen to know where Kurt is, do you?"

"You mean my cousin?"

"That's right."

"How do you even know him?"

Oops. "Oh, I met him at the record store the other day, and we were talking about a festival he was going to try and get me tickets for, but because I was away, I couldn't follow up and I don't want to miss out. I've tried calling both his numbers, but he's not answering."

"He gave you his private number so you could contact him about a festival?"

"I was pretty excited to get tickets."

"You'll have to tell me the line-up later. Maybe I can come, too. Just a sec. I'll see if Chris knows where Kurt is. By the way, how was Sydney?"

"Good," I say brightly.

"Really? I thought you were going to your aunt's funeral."

Shit. Was I? I do remember that trip the first time around, but we often went to Sydney for holidays, so I assumed it was one of those.

"Well, you know, apart from the actual funeral part. It was good to see everyone and be able to grieve properly..."

"You're so weird. Okay, hang on. Chris is here."

She half covers the mouthpiece at her end while she talks to him. After a moment, she comes back.

"Chris said Kurt's at the record store for some album signing with a local band. So, he's unofficially working."

"Oh, okay. Thanks, babe. You're the best. I'll call you tomorrow."

I hurriedly hang up before she can ask me anything else and change into a little black dress. I pack an overnight bag and run back down the stairs. Amy is watching TV like a zombie. Dad is on the phone. Mum is standing in front of the open fridge, looking at its contents.

"All right, I'm off. I'll see you tomorrow," I say to Mum.

She looks up. "Do you need me to make you something to eat before you go?"

"No, I'm fine. Thanks, though. I'll grab something from McDonald's later if I get hungry."

"Okay."

"See you!" I call as I run out to the car.

Phase one of my plan is complete.

***

The drive down to Maroochydore is easy, but my brain is spinning with thoughts of Ed and Maddie's baby, and waking up in 1997 in the sky, and how I'm going to seduce Kurt in a few minutes' time.

I realise I'm going to have to get myself under control if I'm to have any hope of achieving my aim. I can't go in looking desperate and unhinged. Kurt will freak out and try to escape. I take a few deep breaths. In. Out. In. Out.

But it doesn't really help. As I near the record store, it's as though ants are crawling under my skin. I'm so jittery, I almost crash the car when turning the final corner.

I find a car space a little way up the road and get out, walking quickly to the store.

There are people milling around outside, mostly guys and girls in their mid-twenties, all dressed in grunge. I feel self-conscious, knowing I look younger than everyone here. If only they knew the truth.

There's a security guard on the door, and I nervously approach him.

"Uh, hi. I'm here to see Kurt?"

"What's your name?"

"Anna Parnell."

The guard looks down at a clipboard in his hand. "You're not on the list."

"Oh, I'm not here for the signing. I just need to speak to Kurt. Can you please let him know I'm here?"

"Nope."

"Why not?"

"Because my job is to guard the door, not be a goddamn concierge."

"Oh." I try to peek inside, but the guard stands in front of me with his arms folded.

"How can I let Kurt know I'm here?" I ask reasonably.

"Beats me."

"Can I ask someone who *is* on the list to talk to him?"

"I don't care who you talk to, as long as you don't go inside."

"Okay, thanks."

As I turn away, I say *not* under my breath, like the true teenager I'm trying to impersonate.

I look around at the people outside. They either seem to be stoned or banded together in impenetrable cliques.

I try a group of four guys who are loudly debating the merits of Metallica over Pantera.

"Uh, excuse me?" I ask.

They ignore me.

"Excuse me!" I say a little louder.

They all stop and stare.

"Uh, hi. I was just wondering if one of you can go in and tell Kurt that I'm here? My name is Anna."

They continue looking at me for a second and then turn away, going back to their discussion.

Well, that was rude.

I approach another group, two women giggling together.

"Hi. Do either of you know Kurt who works here?"

One of them gives me a death stare. "Yeah, why?"

"I just need to quickly ask him something."

"Why don't you tell me? I'll pass on the message later."

"Actually, I kind of want to ask him in person."

"I'll bet you do. Get lost, kid. He's my boyfriend. He'll never be interested in you."

"Are you Charli?"

She looks disturbed that I know her name. "Why?"

"Oh, I just thought you guys had broken up."

Now I've got her attention. "Listen, you little slut. Don't even *think* about going near Kurt. He's mine, no matter what you think you know. I'd leave now, if I were you."

I stand my ground. "I think I'd like to hear that from his own lips."

"I don't have to justify myself to you, bitch."

"That's really mature."

She looks like she's about to slap me when the security guard comes over. "Is there a problem here, ladies?"

"Not at all," Charli says, giving him a sweet smile.

The guard looks at me. "I hope you're not harassing these women."

"Actually, she is," Charli says. "Do you mind having her removed?"

The guard sighs. "All right. Move along." He starts pushing me down the road.

"I just wanted to speak to Kurt for a second!" I protest.

"Sorry. It's my job to keep the peace. You're not helping."

"Why does Charli get to stay? She was the one calling me names."

"Don't argue with me. Just go, please."

I'm tempted to fight, but I know it's a lost cause.

"Fine," I grumble. I start walking slowly back to the car. I need to think of another approach. Maybe I could stay until the signing finishes. Do they have a back entrance I could sneak into?

And then I realise how ridiculous I'm acting. Obsessed with a guy who won't even know me if he sees me. All because I'm upset about Ed and Maddie. I can't use Kurt as a way to escape these horrible feelings.

I sit down on a nearby curb and bury my face in my hands. I let out a loud sob. What kind of life is this? In love with what is essentially a shadow of the past. This Kurt doesn't even exist anymore.

My brain starts imploding. I think I might be on the verge of a panic attack. My scalp prickles, and my breathing becomes irregular. My chest gets tight as I try to suck in deep lungfuls of air.

I'm not sure how long I sit there, but I'm guessing it's about half an hour later when I hear someone walking along the path behind me.

I ignore them, but they stop.

"Are you okay?"

I jump up and throw my arms around him, not even caring that he doesn't know who I am. Before he has a chance to register what's happening, I kiss him hard on the mouth.

He pushes me away, a bewildered look on his face. "Who are you?"

"Anna. We've met before, but you won't remember." I try to kiss him again, but he steps back.

"Were you talking to Charli earlier?"

"Sort of. But she's not your girlfriend anymore, is she?"

"How did you know that? And how have we met before?"

"It doesn't matter. I'm sick of explaining. Can we just have sex?"

His eyes widen, and he chokes out a laugh. "Um, that's flattering and all, but I don't think so."

"Why not?"

"Because I barely know you. If you maybe told me where we've spoken…"

"At the record store."

"Look, I'm sorry if I gave you the wrong impression when I was at work, but it was unintentional."

"Don't you think it feels like we should have already met?" I push.

He studies my face for a second, although it's kind of dark, so he probably can't see much. "Uh, I guess you do look a little familiar, but to tell you the truth, I'm not into that whole aggressive thing. I just escaped that with my last relationship."

I know I need to reset this whole situation, but I'm feeling a bit out of control, and my brain won't co-operate.

"I'm not aggressive. I just want to kiss you."

"And have sex, apparently."

"Well, yes, that, too."

"Look, I'm sorry. I have to go. Maybe I'll see you around sometime and we can have a proper chat before we get to the physical stuff."

He starts walking away. I run after him and wrap my arms around him, trying to pull his face to mine, but he escapes my grasp.

"Bye, Anna."

I finally let go and collapse back down on the curb.

I start to cry.

EIGHTEEN

I actually end up going back to my parents' house and locking myself in my old bedroom. I'm not tired, but I don't know what else to do, since it's so late and nearly everything is closed.

I lie on the bed and stare at the ceiling. I know I'm solely responsible for the mess I made of the whole evening. I should have handled it better.

I am now super embarrassed and very glad I'll never have to see this version of Kurt again. But I can't bear the idea of Kurt in any reality not liking me.

I get out my mobile and write a text.

Hi, this is Anna. Sorry about tonight. I had some stuff going on. I promise I won't stalk you again.

He doesn't reply straight away. Which is fair enough.

I finally let my thoughts wander back to Ed and Maddie. The discussion I had with Maddie comes back to haunt me about how she wanted kids, just not with the other guy she married. Is that how Ed felt? He couldn't handle the idea of having children with me?

And then I start to analyse my own motivations. Did I not want them with Ed, either? I suppose because he was always working, and when he was around, he was emotionally distant, it was hard for me to imagine us being a balanced family. I didn't want to bring up a child mostly on my own and have Ed find even more excuses to be out of the house.

But if I think about the photo of Kurt in the future, combined with the personality I know here in 1997, I could easily see us as equals, sharing the night wake-ups and diaper changes. I could see him introducing our son or daughter to records.

I let out a little sob. It's all a fantasy. None of that is ever going to happen.

My phone beeps.

I eagerly snatch it up and read the message.

Fuck off and leave me alone.

I let out a surprised squeak. Okay, then.

Message received, loud and clear.

***

I wake up feeling completely wrecked. I wonder if it's because I stayed awake in 1997 until I passed out at 5am and it's now only seven thirty. I had a grand total of two and a half hours' sleep.

I wanted to sleep, but I couldn't. I kept staring at that message from Kurt. It was so harsh. So unlike what I expected from him. Sure, I was a bit of a psycho last night, but surely I didn't deserve that kind of response?

I drag myself to the shower and make the trip over to the café. Kelsey is already there.

"You look awful," she says, concerned. "What's wrong?"

"Nothing." I can't bring myself to tell her about Ed and Maddie, or about how I made a fool of myself in front of Kurt—especially when she advised me not to go back to 1997 until after we opened.

"Are you sure?"

"Yeah. I just didn't sleep well last night."

"Ah. Yeah, me neither. I'm still recovering from our 'trip'—and I also can't stop thinking about this place. My head feels so full."

It's funny that the café is now the one thing I'm not actually worried about. "It'll be fine. We're both professionals. We know what we're doing."

"I know. But it's such a big thing, you know? I don't usually like to put myself out there when there's a chance I can screw up big time."

"We're not going to screw up. The staff are all ready to go, the place looks amazing, and everything is in place. And Saturday is our trial run. Our friends and family won't mind if things aren't perfect. If anything needs improving, we'll have a few days to sort it out before the public arrive."

"Aren't you nervous?"

"Of course. But now more excited than anything."

"I'm so glad I'm going into business with you, babe."

"Right back at ya."

I'm glad she can't see in my head right now and witness the turmoil I'm experiencing in the rest of my life. I need to somehow shut off that part of my brain for a while and focus on this.

If the café is a success, then at least I'll have one positive thing to put my attention on.

And I still have my friends and family. That's all that matters.

***

Fortunately, the rest of the week is busy. Saturday rolls around quickly, and Kelsey and I get to the café at 4pm, ready to greet guests arriving at six.

Our new staff show up an hour after us and get into position, either behind the counter or in the kitchen. Amy arrives next. She looks around at the final touches we made and smiles happily.

"This looks so great. You guys are going to kick ass."

"Thanks, sis. We couldn't have done it without you."

"I know. But I couldn't have done it without your vision."

"Would you like a drink?" I motion to Xander, one of our new wait staff, who brings over a tray of champagne. Amy takes a glass. I take one, too, and swallow half of it in one mouthful. My nerves are starting to get the better of me.

Jackson shows up soon after. He gives me a kiss on the cheek and snatches up a glass as well. I'm so glad that technically, the scene where Kelsey treated him insensitively never existed.

"Congratulations, you two. I'm so proud of you both."

"Aw, you're so sweet."

"I call dibs on the chocolate hazelnut macarons," he says, pointing to the glass case at the counter. "Kelsey brought some of them home last week, and I've been dreaming of them ever since."

I laugh. "I promise one of them has your name on it. Hey, has Kelsey been okay recently?"

"You mean apart from the non-stop manic energy she's been expending in preparation for tonight?"

"Well, yeah. I meant anything out of the ordinary."

He grins and then stops suddenly. "Actually, now that you mention it, she *has* been a little different. She's made me breakfast every day this week and is constantly checking in with me to see if I'm happy. And she bought me this watch, claiming it was an early birthday present." He holds up his wrist, revealing an expensive Georg Jensen timepiece. "I think she's forgotten my birthday isn't for eight more months."

"I think she just wants you to know how much she appreciates your friendship," I offer.

"Aw. She doesn't have to bribe me with gifts to prove that. But I'm not complaining." He squeezes my arm. "You and Kelsey are two of my favourite people."

"I love you, too," I say nudging him in return.

Mum and Dad arrive next. Mum looks a little tired, but happy. I hurry over and find chairs for the two of them.

"This is amazing!" Mum says, wide-eyed. "I can't believe my two babies came up with this!" She looks at the chandelier at the back. "I love that! And those cupcake chairs are adorable."

"Thanks, Mum. I'm so glad you were able to make it. How are you both?"

"Good. We might not be able to stay the whole night, but we definitely had to come and check out this fantastic café!" She eyes off the two food displays. "How did you get everything prepared in time?"

"I had some great staff helping me, but I haven't slept that much in the last few days," I admit. It was good, actually, being so busy. That way, I couldn't dwell on certain people threatening to invade my brain. "Do you want a drink? We have coffee, tea, wine…"

"Just a water, please."

"Me, too," Dad says.

"Done. I'll be back in a moment."

I leave them to go find two glasses that I fill with ice and water. I notice that my kitchen staff need a bit of help as they start to plate up some of the desserts, so I give the drinks to Xander and ask him to take them to my parents.

I'm halfway through smearing strawberry coulis on my fourth plate when I glance back out into the café and notice that Rachel is here. Kelsey goes over to say hello, and they talk for a few moments.

I'm just contemplating whether I should go over, too, when Kelsey squeals loudly and covers her mouth. Rachel looks a little taken aback.

Kelsey grabs her arm and asks her something, but I can't hear what. Then she starts dragging her through the café. "Anna!"

Rachel looks bemused by the whole situation. I reluctantly leave the kitchen and stand behind the counter. I like the idea of having a barrier between us.

"Hey," I say.

"Uh, hey," Rachel says. She gives me a look that I interpret as apologetic but unwilling to admit anything until I make the first move.

Kelsey is bouncing around like she needs to go to the bathroom. "Tell Anna what you just told me!" she demands.

"Why is it such a big deal?" Rachel asks.

"Just tell her. Now! You guys can make up later, but I want to see Anna's face when you tell her."

"Tell me what?" I ask, bewildered.

"Go on," Kelsey says, nudging Rachel.

"Um, you know that night…?"

"I'm assuming you're talking about the last time I saw you?"

"Yes, well Kelsey seems to think you might be interested in knowing a few extra details about the evening."

"You mean like Billy getting food poisoning and being stuck on the toilet for a whole week? Actually, that wouldn't be enough punishment…maybe his penis mysteriously fell off…or…"

"Shut up for a second!" Kelsey roars.

"Sorry, I got a little carried away. What?"

"You know how you told me you kissed someone during the icebreaker?" Rachel says.

"Yes?"

"Was he the last person in line in the second round?"

"Yeeesss…"

"Oh my God! I can't handle the suspense!" Kelsey says, looking like she's about to explode.

"That was my cousin."

My brain short circuits. "Sorry, what?"

"You kissed my cousin, Kurt."

Every cell in my body starts buzzing. I have trouble forming thoughts and getting them out of my mouth. "How? Wh…But…Holy shit!"

I feel faint and lean against the wall, closing my eyes.

Kelsey shrieks with glee. "Isn't that insane?"

"Why are you acting like that?" Rachel asks her.

"Oh, no reason. I think it's just the adrenalin from tonight coming out in weird ways. Anyway, just so she fully understands, maybe you can explain *everything* that happened that night. You guys need to sort your shit out." She whispers in my ear. "Especially if you're going to be related down the track."

I try to swat her but can't get my arm to move.

I kissed Kurt in real life?

Kelsey leaves us alone, and I finally force my body to face Rachel.

"How did this happen? Also, wasn't he living in London with his model girlfriend?"

"He does live in London, but he's back for a few weeks accompanying one of his music acts on tour. He broke up with that model a while ago. The press just haven't caught on yet."

"So, how on earth did he end up at that dark dining restaurant with us?"

"Well, as you know, I didn't realise it was a speed-dating event, and originally I just wanted us all to catch up. Billy is one of Kurt's old friends from when he lived on the coast, and I always had a huge crush on him. He moved to Brisbane a few years back, so when Kurt said he was catching up with him that night, I thought it would be the perfect excuse for me to get to know Billy better, and also see Kurt at the same time. I remember you asked about Kurt that night we were at Shell Beach, so I thought you wouldn't feel too put out by the whole thing. I was never aiming to set you up, but I guess you hit it off anyway."

I can't believe I had the opportunity to spend the whole night with Kurt and I blew it!

"Is he still around?" I ask, holding my breath.

"Oh, no, he's in Sydney now."

I try to hide my disappointment, but I know I don't do a very good job of it.

"But I think he's flying out of Brisbane at the end," she adds. "I can find out for sure?"

"Only if it's no trouble."

She laughs. "You're so crap at pretending to play it cool. That must have been some kiss."

"You have no idea."

And then I think about how just last night he told me to fuck off. I'm still a bit upset about that.

"Hang on a second. I'll be back."

"Okay."

I race off to find Kelsey. She's talking to Amy. "Uh, Kelsey. Can I talk to you for a minute?"

"Sure." We head over to a quiet corner. "The universe is definitely telling you something here," she says.

"I went back to 1997 the other night," I say without preamble.

"Anna! I asked you to hold off until after we opened!"

"I know, I know. But I got some bad news, and I needed to see Kurt."

"Okay, we'll talk about this bad news later—but what happened with Kurt?"

"I tried to have sex with him, and he told me to fuck off."

She laughs. "What?"

I tell her the full story. "So, what if *that* was a sign? That I shouldn't pursue this any further?"

"Um, shouldn't you let the real Kurt be part of that decision?"

"I don't know. He's in Sydney, and I don't even know if I'll get a chance to see him again."

"Well, find out. Don't overthink it."

"But…"

"Stop. Go and finish talking to Rachel. Are you two good now?"

"Uh, actually, we haven't debriefed about Billy yet."

"What are you still doing here, then? Shoo!"

"Okay."

"I need you to be normal in exactly…" She looks at her watch. "…seventeen minutes when we're going to do speeches and have food."

"All right." I go back over to Rachel, trying to stop my thoughts from running away with me. She's still standing where I left her.

"Hey, before we go any further, I just want to say I'm sorry about how all that Billy stuff went down," I tell her.

"No, it's okay. I should have left with you, but I was worried about Kurt. I hadn't seen him in ages, and I didn't want to just ditch him without warning."

"I totally understand."

"And I promise I believed you when you said Billy's advances were unwelcome. I had a bit more of a chat with him later, and he was such a douchebag! I don't know what I ever saw in him."

"So, where did you stay that night?"

"At Kurt's hotel. We chatted about you."

"You did?" My stomach flutters.

"Yeah, he was definitely intrigued by the woman he kissed, and we wondered if it was you. I texted you about it, remember?"

"No! What?" I whip my phone out of my pocket and scroll to the messages from Rachel. Me and my stubborn ways.

There were two messages I didn't read that she sent. The first just says *I'm sorry babe. Are you OK?*

I open the second one.

I'm hanging out with my cousin Kurt, and he wants to meet you. Call me!

"Shit! I didn't read it. God, I'm sorry." Equally for her as well as me.

She laughs. "It's okay. There's nothing you can do about it now."

Agh! I should have made the connection. After all, it was that kiss that made me break my self-imposed time-travel ban and track Kurt down in 1997. But twenty years can change someone. And with the disadvantage of darkness and too much alcohol...

"I'll find out what his plans are. He did tell me he was a bit over London and that he misses Australia."

Holy shit. My heart starts palpitating at the idea of having Kurt back in the same country. And single.

"Please let me know." I wrap my arms around her and squeeze her tight. "Thanks for everything. And sorry about...you know..."

"No problem."

Jackson comes over and throws an arm around my shoulder. "How's my favourite chef?"

"Feeling slightly overwhelmed," I answer honestly.

"That's normal. But you guys have already done an amazing job. You'll definitely do well."

"Thank you."

Kelsey joins us. "All right, woman. I need you now. It's time for speeches."

I beam. "Let's do this."

NINETEEN

The rest of the night passes in a blur of friendly faces, great conversation, and awesome food (even if I do say so myself).

I manage to get through my thank-you speech, but it's as if my body is doing all the heavy lifting for me while my brain drifts off into a fantasy world where Kurt and I are finally together in our proper adult bodies.

At the end of the night, I farewell Jackson. Mum and Dad left just after my speech, so I already said goodbye to them. One of the last people to leave is Rachel. She's driving back to Shell Beach, because she has to work in the morning.

"Thank you so much for coming. I'm glad we sorted everything out," I say.

"Me, too. And I'll keep you posted about Kurt."

"I'd appreciate that."

"Hey, it's the least I can do after the other weekend. Although, if Billy hadn't been such a dick, you would already have been acquainted with Kurt. I know you like him, but it's a lot of pressure to put on each other when you'll only have a limited time together."

"I'll take what I can."

"All right." She leans in and gives me a kiss on the cheek. "Talk to you soon! You guys did awesome tonight. Good luck opening on Tuesday!"

"Thanks!"

Everyone slowly trickles out, and Kelsey and I look at each other with huge smiles on our faces.

"I think we're going to be okay," Kelsey says.

"Me, too," I agree.

"And what a trip, huh? That you kissed Kurt and didn't even know?"

"I probably should have realised. I mean, I know I was drunk, but I'm not normally in the habit of kissing strangers. My body must have known, even though my eyes didn't."

"So, I guess your self-imposed dating ban didn't last long, huh?" she teases.

"I suppose not. But this is different."

"Good. Because I want to see you happy." She thinks for a second. "Did you say earlier that you got some bad news?"

My face falls. "Oh, yeah. I'd actually forgotten about that for a few minutes. Maddie's pregnant with Ed's baby."

Kelsey's reaction is suitably horrified. "You're kidding me!"

"Afraid not."

"What a pair of fucking douchebags."

"To be fair, I don't know if it was planned or not."

"I don't care. I bet they broke the news in a really shitty way, too, huh?"

"In a group phone call," I confirm.

"I knew it. Agh! I'm so mad at them on your behalf." She goes behind the counter and pours the rest of a champagne bottle into a glass and hands it to me. "I wish we had something stronger, but this will have to do."

"This is fine. Thanks, Kels. I'll get over it. In a decade or so." I take a gulp of the champagne. "I mean, it's not like I'm jealous or anything. Just sad that Ed was always the one saying how great it was not having kids. Now I wonder if he just never wanted them with me."

"All I can say is, you dodged a bullet by not having children with him. And just think. Imagine if you *did* get pregnant with Ed and then you split up and found Kurt, and then you'd have to deal with messy custody battles and awkward social situations with the two men in your life."

"You're right." I finish the rest of the champagne. "I'm going to allow myself time to process these crappy feelings and then move on. I have so much to look forward to, and I don't need Ed holding me back anymore."

"That's the spirit."

We start tidying things away. We sent the staff home early as a thank you for performing so well tonight.

"What about you?" I ask as I wipe down one of the tables. "What's going on with your love life? How's Ben?"

"Oh, actually, I think I'm going to call it off with him. I finally went to his house, and I found out he's into taxidermy. There's an actual dead reindeer head mounted above his bed. And he even has this bizarre dollhouse with stuffed rats and guinea pigs playing miniature instruments."

I gasp. "No!"

"I'm afraid, yes."

"And, what? He never said anything until you went to his place?"

"That's right."

"I'm so sorry."

She shrugs. "It's okay. I'm not going to rush into anything else. That trip back to 1997 has made me realise I should start taking things a bit more seriously. Live a life I'm proud of."

"Did you ever call Melanie?"

"Oh, no. I still haven't decided whether I should or not. I was trying to figure out if I'd appreciate a visit from the sister of some guy who did something bad to me, and I'm not sure I would—even if I was a well-adjusted psychiatrist. But at the same time, I want to make sure she knows she's not alone if she ever wants to talk about it."

"I know you'll handle it well if you do decide to contact her down the track."

"Thanks, babe. At least I'm doing one thing right, running this café with you."

"You do a lot of things right. But yes, I think this business was probably one of your better ideas."

I head out into the kitchen and run the sink full of hot soapy water.

I start washing up and think about how funny life is. I thought my experience with the Youth Compound was strange, but it might just turn out that reality is the strangest of all.

***

I crash into bed after midnight and sleep soundly. It's the first time I've felt settled in a while, which is surprising, considering there's a tiny chance I might finally meet Kurt, and my ex-husband is about to become a father. But somehow it feels like everything has turned out the way it's supposed to.

The next morning, Rachel texts me to let me know that Kurt will be back up next weekend to spend his final few days in Shell Beach. Apparently, the DJ he's touring with wants to see where he grew up. Rachel promises to let me know when he arrives and assures me that Kurt is interested in catching up if it fits in with both our schedules. I know that I personally will make every effort to make it fit into mine.

The café officially opens on Tuesday, and within an hour, the customers are lining up out the door. Kelsey did a great job of getting the local media to cover us.

We're flat out all day, and again the next. The third day sees us settle into what is a slightly less frantic pace, but still quite impressive for a brand-new eating establishment.

In the afternoon, just as we're about to close, a familiar face enters.

My eyes widen in surprise.

"Mr. Green?"

He chuckles. "Call me Joe."

"Uh, hi Joe! Welcome to our café! What are you doing here in Brisbane?"

Kelsey is out in the office, so she doesn't know he's here. Yet.

"I was down visiting my brother, and he mentioned this new place that had opened up. He was very impressed with the food, and imagine my surprise when I looked it up and saw who was running it."

"Oh, that's sweet. Here, let me get you something. Would you like a coffee? And maybe a vanilla slice?"

"That sounds delightful."

"Take a seat. I'll bring it over in a minute."

I observe the man standing in our shop. He's actually aged quite well. I'd say he was a little awkward in his early thirties, but now in his fifties, he appears to be a lot more comfortable in his own skin. And he's finally developed some decent fashion sense. Today, he's wearing a pair of black jeans with a well-fitted white T-shirt.

Kelsey comes out to find me. "Anna, I…" She trails off when she sees Joe sitting in the corner. She grabs my arm. "Oh my God! Is that…"

"Yep."

She fans herself. "This is crazy."

"Pull it together," I tease quietly. To Joe, I say, "Joe, you remember Kelsey, don't you?"

He looks up, a genuine smile on his face as their eyes connect. Kelsey is instantly smitten.

I finish making the coffee and point to the vanilla slice. "Kelsey, do you mind serving Joe? I have a couple of phone calls to make."

"Sure," she says, not taking her eyes off him.

I smile and leave them to it.

Maybe a change from toy-boys to someone more mature is exactly what Kelsey needs right now.

Because she deserves someone who cares about her as much as I do.

TWENTY

On Saturday, Kelsey and I have just finished serving the last of the brunch crowd when I get a text.

He's here. He says he can hang around until 2pm, but then he's got a meeting to go to - and he flies out tomorrow. Sorry, babe. I don't know if it's worth still coming?

I almost have a heart attack. Eek!

I think I'll come anyway. I'll leave now! See you soon!

I look at Kelsey. "I have to go."

"What? Right now? He's there?"

"Yep! Not for long, though."

She grins. "All right. Do it! No regrets!"

"No regrets."

I blow her an air kiss and grab my handbag, running out to the car. I set the GPS to give me an estimated arrival time. 1:30pm. Half an hour isn't much, but I'll take it. I just want to see him properly once.

I set up Spotify to play Arctic Monkeys, my favourite driving music, and will myself to relax a little. It's not a short drive, and I don't want to burn out before I get there. The last thing I need is to be a jittery mess and incapable of speech by the time I get to Rachel's. I know what happened the last time I tried to force Kurt into a situation he wasn't ready for.

But within ten minutes, I'm already starting to have doubts about this whole thing. What if Kurt isn't anything like his twenty-three-year-old self?

And yes, we shared an awesome kiss the other week, but it still doesn't take away from the fact I was drunk. And even if my brain *did* interpret him correctly, who knows what the events of the last twenty-plus years have done to him? I know I'm not the same person I was when I was seventeen, no matter how much I like to think I am.

I turn up *Do I Wanna Know* and sing loudly along with Alex Turner. The lyrics kind of fit today.

The drive through the north side of Brisbane is fairly smooth, apart from the usual traffic lights. And the first half-hour of the highway run is clear.

Then, disaster strikes.

My GPS informs me that there is a car accident blocking all northbound lanes up ahead, and there is no way to drive around it. My heart sinks.

As I reach the crest of a hill, I see the long line of stationary cars in front of me, extending far into the distance.

I slow down and come to a complete stop.

Great.

I get out my phone to message Rachel.

Hit a traffic jam. Might be a little late. How's it all going?

She doesn't reply straight away, but I have my messages routed through my car, so they're able to be read by a computer voice when they arrive.

I slam the steering wheel with both hands in frustration. Of course this would happen. On the *one* day I need the road to be clear.

The GPS recalculates my arrival to 1:59pm.

I snatch up my phone again and try some alternate routes, just in case the computer didn't consider some. But no luck. All will get me to Shell Beach after 2pm.

We don't even drive at a crawl. We are literally stopped.

"Your new arrival time is 2:02pm," the GPS speaks again.

"Screw you!" I yell at it.

Maybe the police are just in the process of checking everything's okay and they'll open up a lane soon.

I throw myself around in the driver's seat, probably looking like a maniac to anyone who can see me, but I can't sit still.

People start getting out of their cars and try peering down the road. A few drivers honk their horns. I'm tempted to join them, but I know it won't make any difference.

I watch the minutes tick by with no movement.

"All good here." The robotic car voice reads me Rachel's new message. "What time do you think you'll arrive?"

I don't know. Hopefully just before 2, I write, knowing that saying it won't make it true.

Finally, finally! The cars start crawling along. My body still has the jitters. I don't think anything short of a Valium would calm me down right now.

It takes almost half an hour to reach the place where I assume the accident was, only there's no sign of it by the time I get there.

"Your new arrival time is 2:30pm."

I resist the urge to speed the rest of the way, glancing at the time every thirty seconds. I hope the GPS is wrong, just this once.

But I'm only at Maroochydore by 1:50pm and I know I'm not going to get to Shell Beach in time.

I start to cry. I can't help but wonder if this is a sign. Maybe I'm not supposed to meet Kurt in this reality. Maybe the universe is looking out for me and protecting me from someone I'll be hugely disappointed by if I find out the truth.

A text message comes through ten minutes later.

"He left. I'm sorry. He couldn't wait any longer."

The tears get stronger. I can barely see two feet in front of me, but I keep going until I end up at Rachel's house at 2:30pm.

I'd had my sunglasses on for the drive, so I leave them on and hop out of the car. I ring Rachel's doorbell. She opens it with a sympathetic frown.

"I'm so sorry," she says, giving me a hug. "I know you were excited to meet him."

"Did he say anything about me?"

"He said he would like to see you, but it probably wouldn't work out, because he's leaving tomorrow, and he's going to be tied up for the rest of the day."

I look down at the ground.

"This sucks."

"Come in and have a drink. I really am sorry, Anna. After I found out it was you two that matched at the speed-dating thing, I thought it was super cute…that you had no idea you were both from the coast and connected through me."

I follow her down the hall to the kitchen. "I can't believe I missed him by half an hour."

"Yeah, but it might have been worse if you did hit it off and then he had to leave."

"I don't know." I would have been happy with one minute. I'm sure that would have been enough to know whether it would have worked out between us or not.

She pours two glasses of iced tea and hands me one. "Maybe you need to focus on someone closer to home."

"But didn't you say he was thinking of moving back to Australia?"

"I guess, but that probably wouldn't happen straight away. Sweetie, I don't want you to get your hopes up. You guys shared one drunken kiss.

Kurt is awesome, but he's not *that* awesome."

He really is that awesome to me. At least, he was in the nineties.

"Hey, I have to go to work soon, so I'm afraid I'm going to have to leave you," she says apologetically.

"Oh, of course. Don't worry about me. I'll sort myself out."

"Are you going to be okay?"

"Yeah."

I wish I could tell her how deeply I am affected by this. Kelsey would understand, but Rachel would just think I'm strange.

"I'll keep you posted if I hear anything else."

"Thanks, babe."

It's a beautiful summer afternoon, so I head down to Main Street. I'm going to have a lie on the beach before driving back. At least that will have been one positive thing to come out of the visit.

Main Street is busy. I park in the underground parking and walk through to the beach. I find a spot to sit under a tree near the edge of the boardwalk. I didn't bring my swimsuit with me, so I'm just going to have to admire the ocean from afar.

I watch dozens of happy families splashing around at the water's edge and making sandcastles.

Of course, that reminds me again of Ed and Maddie, and I think of my own feelings towards having kids.

I know when I was a teenager, I always assumed I'd do the traditional get-married-and-have-kids thing and move into a cute house with a white picket fence. But then Ed made our little duo sound so romantic, like we could pick up and head off overseas at the drop of a hat. Which, now that I think about it, we almost never did. We never even got a pet for the same reason, and I definitely would have liked a dog.

Maybe I should look into whether my building allows pets and then visit a shelter. But maybe there's a part of me that's scared of committing to something so permanent.

With that said, I'm definitely not as sure of my decision to never have kids as I once was.

I look out at the ocean and sigh. Hanging around here is pretty, but it isn't doing my mental state any good. I need to return to Brisbane and get back to my life. Actually participate in things I have control over.

I stand up and take my time walking to the parking garage.

I fumble around in my bag for my ticket, resenting that I have to pay for such a short moping session. But I'm just over half an hour, which in the garage's rules is enough time to charge.

There's someone already at the ticket machine, so I wait patiently while he finishes using it.

"Damn it," he says, gently bumping the machine in frustration. I smile. That's how I feel when faced with a larger fee than I expected.

"It's criminal what they charge, huh?" I joke.

He turns around, and I freeze.

Holy shit.

It's him.

He shoots me a cheeky smile, and I almost melt.

"I know, right? Twenty dollars for one hour of parking! I wasn't even here a full hour!"

My brain has trouble processing that this is reality and the universe decided to help me out after all. I also find it difficult to form words. "Uh…yeah…"

His eyes twinkle. "Are you okay?"

I quickly pull myself together. "Sorry, yes. Um, I know this is going to seem weird, but I'm Anna."

His eyes widen. "As in Rachel's friend Anna?"

"The one and only."

He studies me intently for a moment. "You seem really familiar. I mean, apart from the obvious…"

I can't stop smiling. "I know. You do, too."

He holds out his hand. "I should introduce myself properly. I'm Kurt."

I reach out and take his hand. A tornado of energy buzzes between our fingertips. It's just like in 1997, only better.

His skin is a bit more worn, but in a sexy, rockstar-ish way. And those eyes are exactly the same.

I can't help wondering if his lips feel the same. I know we kissed the other weekend, but I want to experience him sober.

He holds my fingers for just a second longer than necessary and then looks at his watch regretfully.

"I'm really sorry, but I have to go. The guys I'm travelling with told me to meet them down here, but then they changed their mind at the last minute." He rolls his eyes. "Creatives."

I laugh. "I can imagine."

"I wish we'd had a chance to get to know each other a bit better…"

I feel like he wants to say more, but stops himself.

"It was great meeting you finally, though," he says eventually.

"You, too," I say, my heart almost in my mouth. This is my last chance.

Just as he turns to leave, I call out. "Hey, what time will you be finished?"

He looks back, amusement playing on his lips. "I'm not sure. Why?"

I can't let this opportunity go. "Do you want to maybe have a drink when you're done?"

He grins. "Uh, sure. As long as you don't mind me not giving you a specific time. I wouldn't want to keep you waiting all night."

"It's okay. My parents live around here, so I can just go hang out with them for a while if I need to."

"Okay. What's your number?" He gets out his phone and hands it to me. I type it in.

He takes back the phone. "I'm sending you a text, so you have my number, too."

"Cool. Thanks. I'll see you later!"

He walks away backwards, watching me and smiling. I probably look like a complete dope as I beam back.

My phone beeps with Kurt's message.

See you soon, Anna.

It's official. I am going on a date with Kurt in real time!

I almost can't handle it!

TWENTY-ONE

I get straight on the phone to Kelsey. "Oh my God, oh my God, oh my God! I met him!"

"You did? I'm guessing it went well?"

"So well! Actually, it was crap at first, because he'd already left when I got to Rachel's, but then I ran into him on Main Street just randomly and he was exactly what I expected!"

I jump up and down, I'm so excited.

"Aw, that's great, babe. What now? I assume he's not standing right next to you at this very moment?"

"Oh, no. He had to go see the guys he's travelling with, but we're going to meet for a drink later!"

"Yay! I'm so happy for you!"

"So, I probably won't be back in Brissie until late, but I'll be in on time to open in the morning."

"Do whatever you have to. If you end up staying out all night, I can always call in someone to cover for you."

I giggle. "Stop! I'm not going to be spending all night with him!"

"You never know. Anyway, have fun and I'll see you when I see you."

"Thanks, Kelsey. You're the best."

"That's true. I am. Talk soon!"

I hang up and look around. I'm still standing near the ticket machine.

What should I do for the next few hours?

I *could* go to Mum and Dad's, like I told Kurt. Only I feel like I'd need to tell them about Ed's baby, and I'm not quite ready to do that yet.

I guess I could go and find a café and just hang out for a while. Or I could buy a swimsuit and actually go for a swim?

"Anna? Is that you?"

I spin around. Who on earth is that? I squint at the man walking towards me. He's tall, skinny, and balding, and he reminds me of an insurance salesman. As he gets closer, I gasp.

"Todd?"

He beams. "Yep. Wow. You look great!"

I stand there awkwardly. I can't say the same of him, and even if it were true, I wouldn't want to. The last time I saw Todd, he practically assaulted me. For a second time. "What are you doing here?"

"Oh, I never left Shell Beach. I own a house up in the hinterland, but I drive in here to work most days."

"What do you do?" I ask politely.

"I'm a real estate developer. We just finalised the contract for a new resort down the end of Main Street. They're knocking down the old building."

So, *he's* one of the reasons Main Street has changed so much in the last twenty-something years. And in my mind, not for the better.

"Cool."

"What about you? Jeez, I haven't seen you since we graduated! When was that? 1997?"

"That's right."

"I assume you're not living around here anymore?"

"No, I'm down in Brisbane."

"That's great. Hey, I have an hour to kill. Do you want to have a coffee or something?"

"Oh, actually, I can't. Sorry. I'm meeting someone else soon."

"No problem. Why don't you give me your number? Next time I'm down your way, I'll give you a call. Catch up on old times."

"I don't know, Todd. You were kind of a dick to me back in high school. Why would I want to re-live that?"

His eyes bulge. "Excuse me?"

"You heard me. You completely ignored me whenever we were out with other people, and all you did was talk about yourself. And then when I called you out on it, you insulted me. So, no thanks. I don't want to catch up on old times."

I'm also still unimpressed by the rum and Coke incident the other night. Even if it didn't occur in this timeline.

"You're still holding a grudge from over twenty years ago?"

I waver. Maybe I am being a bit harsh on the guy. I mean, we all do dumb stuff as teenagers. Maybe he's matured since then.

"I'm not holding a grudge. Sorry, that was uncalled for. Okay, I can fit in a quick coffee."

He looks at me warily. "You're sure?"

"Yes. Come on. You want to go to Beans?"

"Pfft. Beans is a tip. Let's go to Ground."

I vow to reserve judgment. He doesn't have to like Beans. Just because it's one of my favourite places.

"Okay. You're the local."

I follow him a few doors down to a depressingly sterile coffee house. The walls are bare grey blocks, the floor is polished concrete, and you can see all the air-conditioning pipes and plumbing on the ceiling. The front counter has a glass case featuring the same generic caramel slice, carrot cake, and chocolate brownies you see at every other café on the coast. I wish we were in Brisbane so I could show Todd Naughty or Nice and introduce him to real food and coffee. But then I wouldn't want to contaminate the cosy feng shui Kelsey and I are cultivating.

I order a double-shot espresso and sit down next to Todd on an uncomfortably high metal barstool facing the street. None of the tables are set up so that diners can face each other. I know it's a tradition borrowed from Paris, where the chairs are positioned for people-watching, but I never liked that idea. I perch at an awkward angle and sip my coffee. Ugh. The beans are burnt.

Todd drinks his coffee and looks me up and down.

"You've certainly improved with age," he says.

"Thanks," I reply neutrally.

"Not like my wife, Ellie. She peaked in high school."

"Do you mean Ellie who was in our class?" I ask curiously. If it's who I'm thinking of, she was one of the mean girls. And she was very pretty when I last saw her in 1997.

"Yep. I should have known the chick with the curves would just get fatter as she got older."

I look at him, horrified. "Todd! That's your wife you're talking about!"

He shrugs. "She knows she's let herself go. We have four boys, and she seems to have expanded more and more after each one."

I don't care if she was a mean girl at school. No one deserves to have their husband talk about them like that.

"Well, I can imagine looking after four boys wouldn't leave a lot of time to focus on yourself," I reason.

"I should never have gotten married," he muses, ignoring my comment. He then grins at me slyly. "Are you staying in a hotel nearby? Maybe we could sneak away…"

I slam my cup back down on the counter and stand up.

"What kind of deluded world do you live in? No! You are a disgusting human being, and I feel sorry for your wife. You're lucky I don't call her right now and tell her what you just said."

His face darkens. "You wouldn't dare."

I escape to the front door. "You'll just have to wait and see," I call back over my shoulder.

I hurry off down the street and back to my car.

Yuck.

I'm going to have to find somewhere far away to spend the next couple of hours, because I never want to see Todd ever again.

***

I head over to Noosaville and park near The Boat House. I figure an afternoon walk along the river will fill up some of the time before Kurt calls.

If I had run into Todd on any other day, I would have been depressed at the reminder of yet another bad choice I made in relationships, but because I also finally got to see Kurt properly, I'm able to push Todd from my mind almost immediately.

The walk up to the yacht club and back takes less than half an hour, so I sit on a park bench and look out at the river, watching the sky as it starts to take on a warm orange hue.

6pm comes and goes. I check my watch every two minutes until six twenty. I wonder what a reasonable amount of time is to wait. I'd kind of hoped that Kurt would text if he knew he was going to be much longer.

I buy some sushi and eat it without tasting it, constantly checking my phone.

Just after seven, my resolve to wait for him to text fails. I send him what I hope is a breezy message.

Hey, it's Anna. How are you going?

He doesn't reply. It's fully dark outside, and all the restaurants are filling up. I buy myself an ice cream from a nearby gelato shop and sit on the steps overlooking the road, wondering what to do next.

I hope Kurt wasn't just being polite before. Or maybe he had second thoughts once he left. After all, the guy is used to dating models. I know I'm cute, but I'm definitely not model material.

But deep down, I know there's something between us. All those electric first-time introductions couldn't have been a coincidence. I feel like we're supposed to be in each other's lives for real.

At eight, I feel like I have to face the possibility that he's not going to call. I decide to phone him and give him one last chance before I head back to Brisbane. I nervously dial his number and wait. It goes to voicemail.

My heart drops into my toes. So that's it, I guess.

I call Rachel, but her phone also goes to voicemail. Is she with him now, and he's asked her to turn her phone off to avoid any awkwardness? I hope not, but it's possible.

I take my time walking back to the car, giving Kurt one final, final chance.

But no.

He doesn't call.

TWENTY-TWO

The drive home is brutal. I can't help but hold onto the tiniest shred of hope that he'll text or call right up until midnight.

To no avail.

When I get inside my apartment, I drink some warm milk and honey and curl up in bed with a guided meditation. I know I won't be able to fall asleep on my own otherwise.

I head into work the next morning and hate that Kelsey is so excited to see me.

"Tell me everything! I want to know all the details," she demands.

"Nothing happened," I say miserably. "He didn't show up."

Kelsey's face falls. "What?"

"I guess he had a change of heart."

"But…that doesn't seem right. I was sure you guys were meant to be together."

"Yeah, well, maybe not."

"So, he didn't call or anything?"

"Nope."

"Did you call him?"

"He had his phone off."

"Maybe something happened. It might not mean he didn't want to see you."

"But he could have called Rachel to pass on a message or something." I don't tell her Rachel's phone was also switched off, because I don't want her to give me any false hope.

Kelsey tilts her head to the side. "I guess…"

I walk behind the counter and busy myself by checking the fridge for supplies. "I just want to forget about it. The whole thing has gone on way too long. I need to stop deluding myself."

Kelsey frowns. "I don't think you were deluding yourself…"

"Kels, I appreciate what you're trying to do, but it's just making me feel worse."

"Okay. I'll stop talking about it. But if you do need to vent later, or just have a cry, I'm here."

"Thanks."

To be honest, I am *this* close to bursting into tears. If it weren't for the fact that the café only opened a few days ago, I would probably have stayed in bed for a month.

I spend the next hour ordering supplies and planning out the following weeks' worth of food. We've been busier than expected, so I'm going to bring Harriet onboard, who I had on stand-by in case we needed her.

At eleven, my phone rings. I don't recognise the number. A tiny part of me hopes it's Kurt calling from someone else's phone.

I click the *Answer* button. "Hello?"

"Hi, Anna, how are you?"

It's Maddie. My stomach drops.

"About as good as can be expected," I say flatly.

"Can we meet to talk?"

"When you say *we*, who do you mean?"

"I mean me and you." She sounds less confident than the last time I spoke to her.

"Is Ed too scared to face me?" I ask.

"Uh, something like that. Look, can I come see you? I think it will be easier to talk face-to-face."

"I'm kind of working every day at the moment." Even when I'm not at the café, I still have my blog to look after.

"Do you get a break today?"

"I guess I could take half an hour around one."

What's the address of your café?"

"We're just a few doors up from Messina on Melbourne Street."

"Ah. Okay. I'll see you soon. Thanks, Anna."

"No problem."

I hang up. I guess I'm not going to feel any worse than I already do, so today is probably as good a day as any to deal with Maddie. I can't believe Ed would be so spineless, though.

I call Harriet and ask her to come in to discuss her possible new role, and then I head into the kitchen to do some baking. It's good to see that both the 'naughty' and 'nice' halves of the menu are selling equally well. Today, I'm going to start with some bliss balls for the healthy side of the shop. I even got my sponsor to increase the value of my deal, because I have a shelf dedicated to their stuff near the front entrance. It's also selling well, along with copies of my cookbook. It's great to see that the financial and career side of my life is going from strength to strength.

At exactly 1pm, Maddie walks through the door. Kelsey has disappeared, which I'm grateful for. I wouldn't want her making this any more difficult than it has to be. I'm out the back, covered in flour and oil, and I belatedly wish I had tidied myself up. Maddie looks immaculate in a black bandeau dress and heels. Her pregnancy is only just showing.

I don't alert her to the fact that I'm watching her and wait for her to look around the café first. Her expression seems impressed. She approaches the counter and finally sees me through the doorway to the kitchen.

"Hey!" Her face lights up in a genuine smile.

"Hi." I'm confused by this sudden change in attitude towards me.

"This place looks fantastic."

"Thanks."

She points to the tables, which are three-quarters full. "You're busy."

"It will be busier in about an hour," I tell her.

"Then I guess we should get to it."

"Do you want a drink?" I ask.

"Uh, maybe a decaf flat white?" She peers into the two dessert cabinets. "And one of the bliss balls?"

"Good choice." I motion to Emery. "Could you please get us a decaf flat white, a double-shot espresso, and a bliss ball?"

"Sure."

"We'll just be out the back."

I lead Maddie through the kitchen and into a small office. I don't want anyone listening if things get heated. I motion to the armchair in front of my desk. Maddie sits.

"I feel like I'm going for an interview," she jokes.

"Sorry, I just thought it would be better out here…"

"No, no, I totally understand." She studies me for a second. "You look great."

"Really?" I ask, raising an eyebrow.

"Yes! I mean, you obviously have food all over you, and you do seem a little unhappy, but otherwise, you look really good."

"That's nice of you to say."

"I'm sorry for the way everything's turned out."

"You mean, being a bitch to me when I was trying to get my stuff back, and then blurting out the news of your pregnancy on the phone in a smug group call with Ed?"

She nods. "I deserve that. But I need to explain a few things, and then maybe you'll understand why I've been so hostile."

I don't say anything, so she takes it as a sign to continue.

"When I called to tell you the news about being pregnant, I lied to you."

I look pointedly at her stomach. "What's that, then? A food baby?"

She chuckles. "No, no. There's an actual baby in there. But I lied about Ed being part of the call."

I wrinkle my brow. "So, he didn't know you called me?"

"No. He found out the news of the pregnancy the same day you did, and he didn't take it well. I had kind of suspected he wouldn't, so I thought the safest way to tell him would be at work, where he couldn't make a big scene. I don't know if it was the right move because he didn't stick around once he heard what I had to say. He didn't even take his phone with him. I thought maybe he was going to go find you, which is why I called. I figured if I said he was with me and he was actually with you, I would have heard the surprise in your voice, and my suspicions would have been confirmed."

I stare at her. "But he wasn't with me!"

"I know that now. I found out later when he came home, drunk out of his mind to pack his stuff and leave."

My eyebrows shoot up into my hairline. "He left you?"

She nods grimly. "Yep."

"What a fucking coward."

She smiles without humour. "I'm inclined to agree with you there."

"But he left *me* to be with *you*! His true love."

"Clearly, I'm not. At least, not anymore. And to be honest, Anna, he wasn't the man I remembered. Even when he was going through that period after his mum died and he was trying to push me away, I could still feel the warmth he had for me. But when we reconciled after he left you, there was none of that, even right at the beginning. He was like a completely different person. A selfish bastard who only cared about his own needs and wanted me to fit into his schedule."

"I'm so sorry, Maddie. I had no idea…"

"I tried to make it work, but it soon became obvious I was fighting a losing battle. I found out I was pregnant in December, but I didn't want to add to the pressure of Christmas and family and holidays. I knew it would probably be a weird time for Ed, because he would have been thinking of his mum, and it was his first Christmas without you…"

"I take it the pregnancy wasn't planned?" I say gently.

"Definitely not. Ed made it clear up front that he didn't want kids, and I was in the process of figuring out whether that was something I was okay with, when the universe intervened and made the decision for us. My birth control failed."

I instinctively reach out and take her hand. She doesn't pull away.

"And then on New Year's Day, he slept the entire day and night, and when he woke up, it was like he'd experienced some sort of traumatic episode. He kept going on and on about this dream where he was back in 1997, and he saw me when we were teenagers, and then he ran into you, and you helped him when he thought he was having an aneurysm…"

"Did you say 1997?" I ask faintly.

"Yes, why?"

Because it sounds like he took my Youth Compound.

I quickly rearrange my features to something more neutral. "Oh, I was just thinking maybe it reminded him of when his mum died?"

"Maybe. But to me it seemed like he was having regrets about leaving you. So, when you called that day to ask if I had seen that product you were looking for, I wasn't sure if it was just an excuse for you to see each other again."

"No! It definitely wasn't. I promise. I've barely spoken to Ed since we filed for divorce. So, do you know where he is now?"

"No idea. I'm assuming he's holed up in one of those apartments his work pays for, but the office won't give me any information when I call."

"Maddie, I am so sorry this happened." A wave of guilt washes over me. It's all my fault that she's now pregnant and alone.

"Ed is the one who should be apologising and stepping up to the responsibility of fathering a child. But I appreciate your concern."

"Is there anything I can do? Do you have family and friends to support you?"

"Thankfully, I do. And I should have listened to them when I first got back with Ed and they warned me about him. But I was just so excited at having another chance with him…" She trails off, looking wistful despite knowing the eventual outcome.

"I'd like it if we could stay in touch," I say earnestly.

"Oh, of course. I would love that. I know you're a lovely person, Anna, and I would be lucky to count you as a friend."

She jumps up and gives me a hug. I'm caught off guard by the gesture, but quickly recover and hug her back.

I've seen what absentee parenting can do to someone after watching Kelsey have to deal with a broken home, and its fallout on the remaining parent. I want to make sure that Maddie's child never feels that way because of Ed.

Maddie collects herself and starts backing towards the door. "I should go. I know you've got a business to run, but please call me sometime, and we'll have lunch."

"I will."

After she's gone, I slump down in my chair and shake my head. The guilt of being partially responsible for Maddie's pregnancy weighs heavily. And I'm so mad at Ed! What the hell is wrong with him? At least any questions I had about whether we did the right thing splitting up have well and truly been answered.

I sigh. I might have resolved one more issue in my life, but the one I care about most probably won't ever be.

***

I have no idea where Kelsey got to, but she returns soon after Maddie leaves. She opens her mouth, but I start talking first.

"Maddie was just here."

"Really? Why? What happened?"

I tell her the whole story. At the end, her mouth is gaping open.

"Oh my God."

"I know."

"So, Ed accidentally took the compound and thought he was having an aneurysm?"

"Apparently."

She cracks up laughing. "It couldn't happen to a more deserving person."

"Yeah, but who knows if that made things worse? What if that was the reason he reacted so badly when Maddie broke the news of the pregnancy?"

"No, he was always a dick. I'm almost certain that wouldn't have made a difference. Although, hopefully, it made him realise what he's missing out on, now that he's not with you."

"Maybe. Anyway, where were you just now?"

"Just running a few errands." She looks shifty.

"What kind of errands?"

"Stuff."

"What aren't you telling me?"

"Nothing." She pulls her phone out of her pocket. "I just remembered, I have to text Xander to see if he can come in a bit earlier tomorrow and help me work out the next roster..." She walks off, and I watch her, confused. She's hiding something, but I don't know what yet.

I'm kept busy by the afternoon crowd, which is a blessing. There's very little time to think about Maddie's baby, or to remember the feeling of abandonment I experienced last night, sitting by the river.

At 4pm, I start cleaning up, and Kelsey reappears. "Hey, let me do that. Why don't you pretty yourself up a little, and we'll go have a drink at South Bank after we close?"

"You think I need prettying up?" I ask wryly.

She points to a spot an inch above my forehead. "You have something there that makes you look like Mary in *There's Something About Mary.*"

My hand automatically goes to my hair, and I feel a solid chunk sticking straight up. "Ugh, gross. Okay, point taken."

I retreat to the bathroom, where I wash out whatever it is that's glued my hair together. I'm betting it was from the glaze I used in the fruit tarts. Cornflour, sugar, water, and lemon juice.

I wipe the excess flour from my arms and shirt and dab the grease off my face with a paper towel. I touch up my lipstick and evaluate my reflection.

Good enough for a couple of drinks with Kelsey.

I head back out the front and stop when I see who is standing in the doorway.

Kurt.

I quickly shoot a glance at Kelsey, who does a terrible impression of looking innocent. She hurries off out the back, leaving me to face the man who stood me up last night.

He smiles apologetically. "I am so sorry about yesterday. The meeting went way over time, and when the guys could see me looking at my phone every five seconds, one of them snatched it off me and literally threw it in the ocean. So, I had no way of contacting you, and I didn't know your number. I tried calling Rachel to pass on a message, but her phone was off."

"Oh."

"I didn't want you to think I changed my mind about seeing you. But then I kind of figured it was too late. Until Kelsey managed to track me down and invited me to check out your café before I flew out."

"How did she manage that?"

"She went on social media and somehow stalked every act I produce to find out who I was travelling with. It's lucky that my guys posted a photo of the hotel we were staying at, and she recognised it, so she could leave a message for me at reception." He chuckles. "I'm glad she did."

"Oh, good." I know I'm not acting normal, but I feel like I've been put through the emotional wringer these past twenty-four hours.

He looks at his watch and then down at the suitcase on the ground beside him. "Would you like to go have a drink at South Bank? I have an hour before I need to leave for the airport."

"Uh, hang on, I'll just check with Kelsey. I'm not sure if she…"

"I booked a table for two at The Galley," she says, suddenly appearing out of nowhere. She certainly is acting sneaky today.

"You had this planned all along?" I ask.

"Yup. You can leave your bag here, Kurt, and then Anna and I can drop you at the airport after."

"Are you sure? I don't mind catching a cab or an Uber."

"It's totally fine. Go on. Go have your drink."

Kurt raises an eyebrow at me as if to ask *are you okay with all of this?*

"It's definitely no problem dropping you at the airport." I motion towards the door. "Shall we?"

Kurt follows me outside. I quickly mouth a *thank you* to Kelsey through the window. She pretends to make out with an imaginary person, and I have to stifle a laugh.

"You own that café?" Kurt asks, looking at the sign above the door.

"Yep. With Kelsey. I do all the cooking, and she looks after front-of-house."

"I really like it. I wish I was around longer so I could try some of your food."

"If you're lucky, I might give you some to take with you to the airport," I tease.

"I'd like that."

We walk in silence for a couple of minutes. I don't even know where to start. There's so much to cover in such a small amount of time. And then what? He's back to London for who knows how long.

"How has it been living in London?" I ask.

"Oh, I've loved it. There's no way I could have achieved half the stuff I've done if I'd stayed on the coast. But the weather is nowhere near as nice. And I do miss how laid back it is here."

"What are your plans once you go home?"

"I guess wind up the rest of the shows with the guys and then move onto the next project. I haven't really figured it out yet."

I want to ask him if what Rachel said is true, and whether he is considering moving back, but it's too soon.

"What about you?" he asks. "What are your plans?"

"I guess I'm sort of tied to Brisbane for a while. We only just opened the café, and I want to see where it goes. But I don't really have many other plans at this stage."

We reach The Galley, and the waiter seats us at our reserved table, looking out over South Bank's man-made lagoon.

I order a glass of Prosecco, and Kurt orders a beer. He sits opposite me and studies me for a second.

"Why do I feel like we've done this before?" he asks.

"I don't know," I smile. "Maybe we met in another life."

"I wonder if it's because we both grew up in the same area."

"It could be."

Or it could be that you're channelling one of the other realities where we've spent time together.

Our drinks arrive, and I sip mine. "How did you get that scar?" I ask, pointing to the mark above his eyebrow. It's the one I felt the other weekend at the speed-dating event.

"Oh, it was a long time ago. I dated this girl called Charli who was really intense. I broke up with her, but she was reluctant to let go. I was helping out at an album launch at a record store in Maroochydore, and she was there causing trouble. I asked her to go home, but she followed me back to my place and we argued. Things kind of escalated, and she threw a bottle at me."

I stare at him, horrified. "She threw a bottle at your face?"

"Yeah, it was pretty bad. I had to have a ton of stitches. But I never saw her again after that night."

"What year was that?" I ask, trying to sound casual.

He thinks for a second. "It must have been the summer of 1997."

It's too much of a coincidence to think that there was another album launch in early 1997 where Charli caused trouble. And if so, could it have been her who told me to fuck off in that text message? It would make sense.

I smile, and Kurt looks confused. "Why are you smiling?"

"Sorry, I'm not smiling at your injury. I was thinking about where I was around that same time. If you're talking about the record store on Duporth Avenue, I often shopped at The Palace across the street."

"Weird, huh? And then we reconnected at that restaurant…" He trails off, possibly remembering our kiss.

"I…" I start to say, but Kurt starts talking at the same time.

"Sorry, you go," he says.

"No, you first," I say.

He laughs. "I was just going to say, I hope this doesn't sound creepy, but that kiss…" He shakes his head.

"What?" I ask playfully.

"It was pretty damn memorable."

I grin. "I agree." And then my insecurities get the better of me. "Rachel mentioned you were dating someone back in London?"

"Oh, not for ages. I was sort of seeing someone called Olivia, but it was too hard to make it work. Our schedules never aligned. And I found when we did have a week off with nothing planned, we'd just argue. We broke up around the end of June last year but didn't make it official until a few months after that. Olivia wanted me to go to a few events with her that I'd previously agreed to, so I stuck to my promise."

I swallow. The end of June? This is getting spooky. That's when I broke up with Ed.

I gulp down the rest of my Prosecco. "Do you think you'll ever live in Australia again?" I blurt out.

"You know what? I was actually thinking about that yesterday. After being back at Shell Beach and spending some time with the guys, it reminded me of all the great memories I had there. I have enough money now to do what I want, so it's a possibility."

I laugh nervously. "Sorry, I know this situation is kind of weird. I mean, you don't normally kiss someone before you meet them."

His eyes twinkle. "That's true. And you don't normally have a first date right before being separated for an indeterminate amount of time."

At least he's calling it a date. I like that.

"So, what now?" I ask.

He sighs. "I'm not sure. I would love to see you again, but I don't know how we can make it work."

"I know what you mean."

"And while I may decide to move back here at some point in the future, it probably won't be in the next few months. I wouldn't want to put that kind of pressure on you."

"Yeah."

"Let's just forget about that for the moment. We have…" He looks at his watch again. "…twenty minutes before I have to go, so let's just talk. I want to know as much as I can about you in that time."

I smile sadly. "Okay."

The time passes way too quickly. Kurt and I barely scratch the surface of our lives, covering families, career trajectories and in my case, my marriage.

"Wait, when did you split up?" he asks.

"June last year," I admit.

"That's an interesting coincidence," he says.

"It is a bit."

Imagine what he'd think if he knew everything.

Kurt stands up and reaches his hand out to me. I take it and allow him to help me to my feet, but he doesn't let go when we go over to the counter to pay for our drinks and walk back up the street.

"I'd really like to stay in touch, Anna, but I understand if that doesn't work for you."

"It works for me," I say, smiling.

Just before we reach the café, Kurt stops. He leans against a nearby brick wall and pulls me into him. "I need to see if last time was a fluke," he says, looking at my mouth.

"I'm all for a bit of experimentation," I murmur, as I press my lips to his.

And it's the best parts of every kiss we've already shared, all rolled into one big ball of super-charged sexiness.

He gently strokes my hair as his mouth explores mine. I don't want to let him go.

"Sorry to break this up, but Kurt, didn't you have to be somewhere?" Kelsey's voice interrupts us.

We reluctantly pull apart, Kurt with a lazy smile on his face, and me with flushed cheeks.

"Maybe I could change my flight," he says.

"Well, decide now, because I have stuff to do if you don't need my car."

Kurt looks at me and I can see the longing. "I want to…"

"But it would just be putting off the inevitable," I reason.

"You're right. Okay. I suppose we should go."

Kelsey hands Kurt a small plastic container containing a mini mudcake. "You can have this to remember Anna by."

He takes it, laughing. "Thank you."

"Anna, do you want to lock up, and I'll help Kurt put his suitcase in the car?"

"Sure." I head over and turn the key in the lock before pulling down the security door and locking it, too.

I head back over to the car.

"You can drive," Kelsey says, handing me her keys. "And Kurt, I'm letting you sit in the front passenger seat, just this once."

"Thanks, Kelsey," he says, appreciatively.

"You can drop me off at home on the way, and then Anna, I expect you to bring this car home safely."

"I'll treat it as if it were my own."

We drive via the Valley, where Kelsey lives with Jackson, and she waves to Kurt. "It was great meeting you! I hope it's not the last time I get to see you!"

"Me, too. Thanks again, Kelsey."

Kurt and I drive in silence for a few minutes.

"This is a bit weird, isn't it?" I say eventually.

"Yeah, I guess. Considering we really only met properly yesterday. Unless you count…"

"I'm sorry I didn't hang around at the speed-dating thing. It wasn't a great night for me. I'd had a lot to drink, and then I had a bit of a disagreement with Billy…"

"Rachel told me. I am so sorry about that. I sort of hold myself responsible. Billy used to be a good friend, but he's changed a lot in twenty years. And not in a good way. At all."

"You weren't to know."

"No, but if I hadn't brought him along, maybe we would have had a bit longer to get to know each other."

"It's over now. We'll just have to make the best of it."

Once at the airport, I pull into the drop-off zone and get out to say goodbye. Kurt wraps me up in a huge hug, and I cling to him as if I'm never going to see him again. Which, in the back of my mind, I realise is a distinct possibility.

"I know it was way too short, but I'm still glad we got to do this," he says.

"Me, too."

He kisses me softly. I want to remember every single second.

A taxi honks at us, wanting to get into our space.

I hold up a finger to say I'll just be a second, but the moment is over. Kurt drags his bag towards the door, looking back at me with a mixture of longing and regret. It's exactly how I feel.

"Bye, Kurt," I whisper.

"Bye, Anna," he calls back.

I get back in the car and drive away, feeling empty.

TWENTY-THREE

I feel out of sorts for the next few days. Kurt is in transit for the first two, so I don't even get to talk to him until Wednesday. Even when we finally do, I can already feel the immense distance settling in between us. It's hard to remember what I'm supposed to already know about him, and what I learned from visits back to 1996 and 1997. I can tell he wants to get to know me better, but he's busy with work, and the time difference makes it difficult for us to understand each other. If I'm organised, I can catch him just before I go to work, and before it gets too late at his end. Or I can talk to him after I get home in the evening, but it's early there.

By the end of the week, I'm questioning whether I should have bothered meeting him at all.

On Saturday morning, Kelsey shows up at my place at 6am. She rings my mobile to wake me up and demands to be let in.

I answer the door, rubbing my eyes. "What on earth are you doing here this early?" I ask.

"I've decided you're going to go back to 1997."

"What? Why?"

"Because I've seen how bummed you've been the last few days. You need a bit of fun in your life!"

"I don't know…it feels kind of irresponsible."

"I'll look after the café, so don't worry about that."

"Are you sure?"

"Yes! You have more chance running into Kurt there than you do here."

"But it's not the same version of him."

"Does it matter?"

"Yeah, it does."

"Just do it."

"I don't know. It would feel weird. Almost like I'm cheating on the real Kurt with a lesser version of him."

"That's the dumbest thing I've ever heard. If you wanted to find the other me there, I wouldn't be offended. I'd think it was cool. In fact, look me up and hang out with me today, and then report back tomorrow."

I laugh. "Okay. Thank you. I really appreciate you looking out for me."

"Hey, that's what besties are for. But before you find me, why not go to Kurt's place this morning? I'm sure you could come up with a great excuse to convince him you need to spend some time together?"

"Maybe I will."

I mix up a dose of the compound and drink it before I have a chance to overthink the situation any further. I lie down and close my eyes. I am actually quite looking forward to a day of escapism. And even getting to see Kurt again. I know he won't remember me, but at least he'll still know who I am once I wake up. Just minus whatever we talk about today.

It's an overcast, humid morning in Shell Beach in 1997. I get up and look out the window. The clouds are hanging low in the sky, and everything is grey. Not ideal, but at least it's not raining. I have a quick shower, put on a little polka-dot dress, and sneak downstairs.

Everyone is still in bed, so I leave a note saying I've gone out and grab the car keys.

The road isn't too busy, and I get to Maroochydore just after 7am. It's probably a bit early to knock on Kurt's door, so I go to a nearby shop and buy a bottle of orange juice to drink down at the river.

I've decided when I see Kurt, I'm going to use the same story I went with last time and ask him if I can borrow a few albums for a party at Rachel's.

At 8am, I knock on the front door and wait.

After a moment, it opens, and he's standing there. He doesn't say anything for a moment, and just stares at me. My brain goes blank, and I totally forget my story.

"Uh…hi…"

"Anna?"

My eyes widen. "You know who I am?"

He looks a little shell-shocked, but nods.

"How?"

"I think maybe you should come in and talk to my guest. I have a lot more questions of my own."

I step inside. Kelsey is sitting on the couch. "Surprise."

"So, you decided to come, too?" I ask. "Why didn't you tell me? And what about the café?"

"Don't worry about the café. That bit's been taken care of. And I didn't tell you I was coming here because I wanted to arrive first and make sure that this…" She points to me and Kurt. "…happened smoothly."

"Can someone please explain to me what's going on?" Kurt asks, confused.

"Ah, yes. Sorry." Kelsey turns to me. "Anna? Do you want to do the honours?"

"Oh, um, we're friends with Rachel, and we were hoping to borrow some albums for a party we're having…"

Kelsey laughs delightedly. "You went with the same story as last time.

217

Excellent. I mean, why bother reinventing the wheel, huh?"

I give her a warning look. Kurt looks at me, dazed. "So, is this a dream, or what?" he asks.

"We don't think it's a dream," Kelsey explains. "But if it makes it easier for you to comprehend, by all means, call it that."

I gape at Kurt. "Wait, what? What do you mean by 'is this a dream?'" I turn to Kelsey. "What did you do?"

"Okay, well I guess now that you're both here, I should explain a few things."

"Please do," I say, nervously watching Kurt. He keeps looking around the living room as if he's seen a ghost.

"All right, so Anna, I brought future Kurt back here. I figured it was the perfect way for you to get to know each other better, even though you're living in separate countries. And also, he'll believe you when you tell him everything else."

My brain is scrambled. "But...how? How on earth did you pull that off?"

"It was actually easier than I thought. You know that cake I gave Kurt to remember you by?"

I nod.

"I put a dose of the compound that I stole from your jar in the middle of it, and then I wrote a note saying he wasn't to eat it until Friday night."

"Didn't you think that was weird?" I ask him.

"A little. But Kelsey came up with a really convincing story about how the French wait a few days to eat their desserts, because it gives the flavours a chance to fully blend together." He thinks for a second. "Although, now I say it out loud, it sounds pretty silly to have to wait for a specific time."

Kelsey waves a hand dismissively. "Anyway, I've started to explain to

Kurt what's happening, but I thought I'd leave the rest of it up to you. Now that you're here, I can go. Have fun! And I'll see you, Anna, tomorrow."

She skips off, whistling to herself.

I'm still standing in the doorway, dumbfounded.

Kurt flops down on the couch. "What's this compound Kelsey's talking about? Is it LSD or something?"

"No, no. It's not like anything else out there. As far as I'm aware. I got it from the supplement company that sponsors me. It allows you to spend twelve hours in 1997."

"Why 1997?"

"I don't know. Last year, it took me back to 1996."

He looks overwhelmed. "So, we're actually time travelling?"

"Sort of. But nothing we do here will change the future, so you don't have to worry about that."

He smiles dryly. "Oh, that's okay, then."

"I'm sorry Kelsey tricked you into doing this. I would never have let her if I knew…"

"Okay, wait. Start at the beginning."

I take a deep breath. "You really want to know?"

"I have twelve hours here, don't I?"

"I guess you do."

"Then yep. I want to know."

I cautiously enter the living room and sit down beside him.

"Last year, this supplement showed up in one of my deliveries, and when I took it, I blacked out and woke up in 1996. Most of the day was the same as the first time around, except for one thing. I met you."

I can't read his expression. "Really."

"Yep. You were working at the record store, and you took me into the back room and played *Sad-Eyed Lady of the Lowlands* to prove that vinyl sounds better than CD or cassette."

He laughs, surprised. "That *does* sound like something I'd do."

"I've been back here nine times now, and every time I visit, I end up seeing you—and almost always randomly."

"Is that right?"

"You don't believe me?"

"I don't know what to believe." He waves his hand around the living room. "I mean, I'm here, aren't I? This is clearly an exact replica of the place I rented back in 1997."

"It's not a replica. It's the real thing."

"If you say so. Then what happens now?"

"I don't know. Is there anything you'd like to do? I can leave you to explore on your own if that would make you more comfortable…"

"No. Don't leave."

"Okay, I won't."

"I should have known there was something weird with that cake. The middle was purple, and it tasted like chlorine. I was kind of disappointed that your cooking didn't live up to my expectations," he says, lightly teasing.

"Do *not* judge me on that. I promise my cooking is amazing. Are you hungry? I can make you something now?"

"Uh, I don't remember ever having much food in my cupboards, so you might be hard-pressed to locate the ingredients you need."

I go over to his kitchen and open the fridge. "You have the basics…eggs, butter, milk. Let me make you breakfast, and we can talk more."

"I just had dinner in London."

"Well, it's breakfast time here, so I'm afraid you're going to have to deal with it."

He chuckles. "Point taken."

I decide to make French toast and quickly go back to the shop where I bought my juice to purchase a thick-sliced loaf of bread.

"Tell me about the other times we met here," he says when I return. He makes his way around the living room, occasionally picking up a book or furnishing and marvelling at it.

"Um, there was one time when you were playing Frisbee and fell on top of me at the beach."

He laughs. "I was always smooth like that."

"And there was the time we had an early dinner together at Sizzler and you were surprised I liked seafood, because none of your friends did."

He nods, as if what I'm saying rings true.

"And you told me on a Monday night at the end of June that the Jewel Box constellation would remind you of me from now on."

His eyes widen.

"Apparently you got a tattoo of it the next day," I confirm.

He slumps down onto the floor. "This is insane."

"I know."

"How…um…how far have we…?"

"We haven't slept together," I reassure him. "Although, I did try one time, and you weren't impressed. Granted, you were still dealing with Charli. Actually, it was the same night that she gave you that scar."

"Holy shit."

"Sorry, I know this must be a lot to take in. How about we just have breakfast and forget about the fact we're in 1997 for a while?"

"How can I forget that? Just looking at you reminds me of where we are!"

I hand him a plate of food. "Here. Maybe eating will make you feel a bit more normal."

He takes it and eats it slowly. Despite what I'm sure is a ton of information to process, he smiles.

"This is pretty good."

"Does it make up for the mudcake Kelsey contaminated?"

"Almost."

I don't say anything for a while, letting him eat and think. I mindlessly flick through his albums in the crate on the floor and spot the Stone Temple Pilots' album *Core*. I slot it into his CD player and skip to the song *Plush*.

He looks at me. "I suppose it's no coincidence you picked that song."

"Nope. And there's another song I introduced you to once that you really liked."

"What's that?"

"*Darkness*."

That seems to be the clincher for him. He finishes eating and crawls over to sit beside me.

"Anna, I have no idea what's happening here, but it feels like the universe is trying to tell me something. And I don't want to ignore it."

My heart starts hammering.

"What does that mean?"

He gently strokes my face. "It means I want to see where this goes. And if we have to meet back here in 1997 to actually spend time together, then so be it. I don't suppose you can send me some more of that compound in the mail?"

"I'll see what I can do," I laugh.

He leans forward and gently kisses me.

"I can't wait to get to know you better, Miss Anna."

"And I can't wait to learn more about you. I know almost nothing of your life after 1997."

"That's a relief." He kisses me again. "It would be disappointing if you already knew *everything* about me. How about we spend the day showing each other our lives here, and we can catch up on the future at the same time?"

"That sounds perfect."

He helps me to my feet and takes my hand.

"I know we haven't been acquainted long in my memory, but this feels right. And it might sound weird, but I can't think of anyone else I'd rather choose to embark on this crazy adventure with.

I squeeze his hand.

"I feel the exact same way."

THREE MONTHS LATER...

"Come on! We'll be late for the show!"

Rachel is hustling us up the street towards The Triffid in Newstead. I've never seen a gig at this particular venue, but I'm looking forward to experiencing it for the first time. Jackson and his partner Cash are beside me, and Kelsey is tagging along behind with Joe, who is down visiting for the weekend. I have to keep reminding myself not to call him Mr. Green. I'm loving that he and Kelsey seem to be besotted with each other. Joe won't reveal how he felt about Kelsey back in high school, claiming he never saw students in a romantic way, but he has hinted that out of everyone he taught, she stuck in his mind the most.

I glance back and see Kelsey whispering something in his ear. He laughs.

"What are you up to?" I ask her.

"Nothing. Well, nothing you'd be interested in. Unless you want to know the colour of the lingerie I purchased from Victoria's Secret today?"

I wrinkle my nose. "Please, no."

"See? Not everything revolves around you, Anna," she teases.

"Yes, but tonight I feel like I'm way out of the loop. You all seem to know what we're doing, but for some reason you don't want to tell me!"

"You'll understand why soon."

I look at Rachel. "This isn't going to be like that dark dining experience, is it?"

"No, no. But, um, aren't you forgetting a certain cousin of mine you kissed that night?"

I sigh sadly. "Don't remind me."

I'm so happy to be out with my friends tonight, but I really wish Kurt could be here, too. He's still in London, although he is definitely making plans to move back to Australia before the end of the year. We continued to catch up in 1997 once a week for a little while after Kelsey first drugged him, but the compound started to run low, and I wanted to save a few doses in case of an emergency. What kind of emergency might require a visit to 1997, I'm not quite sure, but you never know.

It feels like forever since I've had any physical contact with him. We talk on Skype, but it's not quite the same.

"You know, Kurt is really excited to move back and be with you," Rachel says. "He just has to wind up all his commitments in the UK first."

"I do know. I'm just impatient."

We arrive at The Triffid, and Rachel hands the security guard my ticket so I can't peek at who we're seeing. The outside wall is covered in posters for upcoming gigs, but I don't get a chance to examine them all before I'm dragged inside.

We find a couple of bar stools down near the front, and Joe goes off to buy the first round of drinks.

Kelsey sits near me. "I was talking to your sponsor earlier."

"Oh? What about?"

"About whether I could ask someone in product development about a particular compound they might have accidentally given you."

"Really? What happened?"

"Well, I had quite a weird chat with one of the scientists at their lab. From what I can gather, the people in product development are allowed to spend a portion of their work hours on new ideas, you know like how some tech companies let their employees do that with coding?"

"Okay…"

"And so, the guy I ended up talking to had been working on a drug that was supposed to induce lucid dreams, only he was shut down before he had a chance to test it properly. Apparently, the company saw it as a frivolous endeavour, and not in line with their branding."

"Did you ask him how we ended up with it?"

"Yeah, he admitted he wanted to see what happened if people took it, so he made up a few batches and planned on sneaking them into deliveries. Only he had a change of heart at the last minute and decided not to. He thinks maybe someone picked one of them up by accident when they were making your pack. For the record, he's very interested in talking to us about our experience."

"I'll bet."

Huh. So, the youth compound might be a replicable product. I wonder if I could bribe the scientist to make me some more, in exchange for using me as a guinea pig?

Joe returns with some drinks and hands one to each of us.

My phone beeps. It's Maddie.

Hey, babe. How's the show? So jealous you're there without me.

I type back, smiling. Maddie is now part of our gang, but she couldn't make it out tonight. The second trimester of her pregnancy is causing her to throw up almost constantly, especially at night.

It hasn't started yet, and I still don't know who we're seeing. Don't worry, you'll be back out partying in no time. I'll babysit for you whenever you need me.

I take a sip of my drink and glance at the stage. It looks like the show might be starting soon.

Aw, you're so sweet. Thanks, honey. Keep me posted on the rest of the night. I'm sure I'll be awake and puking for at least the next five hours, so feel free to text anytime.

Neither Maddie or I have heard from Ed since the day he learned of the pregnancy, but we have both agreed it's probably for the best. After sharing stories of our time with Ed, we realised just how selfish and narcissistic he really was. Maddie even started to question her time with Ed when they were teenagers, wondering if she'd been too young to know any better.

I'm just starting to reply to Maddie's text when the lights go down, and a cheer reverberates around the room.

Two people walk out onto the stage. I squint, but I can't see them clearly. They both step behind a massive DJ console and put on headphones. A few seconds later, a familiar song starts pumping through the speakers.

Darkness. By Larkin.

An extended intro plays while one of the guys starts to speak.

"Good evening, everyone. I'm so glad you could make it out to see us tonight. This is our first show after a fifteen-year hiatus, but we are stoked to be back, and we owe it all to the amazing Kurt Hamilton. After he very kindly mentioned us in an interview last year, there was a massive renewed interest in our music. So, after writing to Kurt to thank him, he convinced us to get back in the studio, this time with him, and make some new tunes that we think you're going to love. But first, this one is for Anna!"

The bass kicks in, and the song starts for real. My heart bangs along with the beat. I stare at Kelsey and then Rachel, who grin at me.

And then someone taps me on the shoulder.

I spin around.

I should have known.

I jump into Kurt's arms and kiss him hard on the mouth.

He laughs. "That was some welcome."

"That was some song dedication."

"I'm glad you like it."

"What are you doing here? How come you didn't tell me?"

"I wanted it to be a surprise. I actually started planning my permanent return to Australia right after I left you, but I wasn't sure how long it would take. But after we stopped being able to see each other in 1997, I worked even harder to speed things up. I hate not being with you."

"Me, too."

"I have Kelsey and Rachel to thank for organising everything back here and making tonight possible."

I glance over at the two of them. They're both beaming.

"Thanks, guys," I sing-song.

"You're welcome."

I look back at Kurt. He's watching me with a small smile.

"What?" I ask self-consciously.

"I'm just so happy to be here with you, in real life."

"You're not missing my seventeen-year-old body?" I tease.

He laughs. "Ah, no. To be honest, it made me feel like a dirty old man when we were together in 1997. But now..." He gently puts me to my feet and strokes my face. He leans forward and kisses me again. "I love you, Anna Parnell."

I softly sweep my finger across the scar near his eyebrow. "I love you, too, Kurt Hamilton. No matter what age you are."

"Good. Because I still want to be with you, even when we're eighty. Or one hundred."

"And when we're too old to walk, we can always take the compound and hang out in a time when we could still move."

"My head hurts just thinking about going back in time to a point in the future."

We both turn to the stage, holding hands and watching the rest of the song that inspired Kurt's music career.

And it was all because of a bond that couldn't be broken, no matter the timeline.

We were meant to be.

Thanks for reading *1997!*

I really hope you enjoyed it. If you'd like to get in touch, I can be found on most social media and book-related websites. Reviews on your preferred platform are always appreciated, as are personal messages.

Also, if you'd like a FREE copy of *Before Coco Bay*, sign up to my newsletter at https://www.kirstymcmanus.com.au/get-free-stuff/

Read on for a sample of *1998* and a list of my other books.

Kirsty.

Facebook: /kirstymcmanusauthor
Instagram: /kirstymcauthor
Goodreads:
https://www.goodreads.com/author/show/5434523.Kirsty_McManus
Bookbub: @KirstyMcManus
Web: https://kirstymcmanus.com.au

ONE

Have you ever been so happy that you worry life can only go downhill from here? Because I've been feeling that way for a while now, and I'm sort of waiting for the bubble to burst.

Even tonight is so perfect, I can't imagine another New Year's Eve ever topping this one. I'm here with all the people I love, and we're celebrating at a venue that was borne out of a friendship going back decades.

Kelsey is halfway through taking a sip of sparkling wine, but I spontaneously reach out and wrap an arm around her shoulder. "You're an amazing woman, Kelsey Gillespie."

She half-chokes as she tries to swallow her mouthful. "Right back at you, Anna Banana."

I glance over at Kurt, and he smiles at me from the other side of the room. I grin back and blow him a kiss. He pretends to catch it.

Kelsey sees our PDA and groans. "You guys make me sick. I can't believe how lovey-dovey you still are."

"Sorry," I sing-song, not feeling even remotely apologetic. "Surely you understand what it's like. I mean, you and Joe still act like teenagers."

"Not around other people, though."

"Really? Because I swear I saw you doing that tongue thing earlier. It reminded me of Pamela Anderson and Tommy Lee's wedding back in 1995."

She giggles. "You weren't supposed to see us. We were trying to be discrete."

"I don't know how you possibly thought that. You were standing in the middle of the kitchen while I was attempting to pour drinks. And for the record, it still weirds me out that you're having sex with our old chemistry teacher."

She rolls her eyes. "Get over it. But you have to admit, he is a total hottie."

Joe Green is sitting on the couch, deep in conversation with Jackson and his partner, Cash. Admittedly, Joe does look great these days, and his clothing and hair are very on-trend—but every now and again, I'll have a flashback of him reprimanding me as a teenager, and I can't imagine Kelsey not having similar memories.

I glance at the clock on the wall and see it's only a couple of minutes until midnight. We chose our café, Naughty or Nice, for our New Year's Eve celebration, figuring it was a convenient location for everyone to meet. We'll be closed tomorrow, so Kelsey and I knew we could leave any mess until we'd recovered from our hangovers.

"We should get ready for the countdown," I tell her.

She looks at the clock, too. "Wow, that went fast." She goes over to the speaker and turns down the music, which happens to be Run DMC's *It's Like That.* Tonight's theme is the nineties, but I swear I had nothing to do with the decision. It was actually Jackson who suggested it when Kelsey and I were sending out the invites. Kelsey thought the idea was hilarious and begged me to agree. I'd had enough of the nineties to last me two lifetimes, but I didn't want to look like a party pooper. So, tonight, I'm dressed in a long navy polka-dot dress a la Gwen Stefani in the *Don't Speak* music video, complete with chunky Doc Marten boots and black plastic bracelets.

Kurt is dressed like his namesake from Nirvana, in torn jeans and a black and white horizontal-striped shirt. It doesn't look wholly different from the stuff he normally wears, and I always joke that his fashion sense stalled in the decade where I first met him.

"Hey, everyone," Kelsey calls out. "We have just over a minute until midnight. Make sure your glasses are full and you're close to whoever you're going to make out with to ring in the new year."

Kurt raises an eyebrow at me suggestively. I still find him ridiculously attractive, but then it's only been eight months since he moved back from the UK. In that time, I've been busy establishing the café, and he's been working with a local artist on their new album.

I blush and hold out my hand, gesturing to him with a finger.

He holds up his glass and nods at mine. It appears they're both empty. We meet at the counter, and he pours some more wine.

"Are you having a good night?" he asks.

"I am. You?"

"Yeah. It's nice to get everyone together."

As the clock ticks down to twelve, I look around. Kelsey and Joe are already groping each other in one corner. So much for being discrete. Jackson has his arm around Cash, and they seem blissfully happy. Rachel and her brother Chris are chatting animatedly. Chris is back from Thailand for a few weeks to see his family, Kurt included. And my sister Amy is leaning against the back wall, laughing at something her friend Stacey said. They're both between relationships at the moment.

"…5-4-3-2-1! Happy New Year!"

The fireworks at South Bank crackle outside. I turn to Kurt, and he pulls me in to his chest, lifting my chin so he can kiss me. I sigh with happiness. I don't think I will ever tire of kissing this man. His lips are made for mine.

"Happy New Year," he says softly.

"Happy New Year to you, too." I wrap my arms tightly around him. "Do you have any resolutions?"

"I don't know. Things are pretty good right now. I guess I'd like to finish the new music project. And have some adventures with you."

"Sounds good. I'm feeling the same. I just want to keep the café ticking along and maintain my blog. My online stuff is going better than ever, and my publisher has asked if I can put together a concept for a new recipe book. Everything seems to be balanced perfectly."

Kelsey comes over and shoves her body in between the two of us. "I love you guys," she says magnanimously. I think she's had more alcohol than any of us.

"We love you too, Kels."

"Hey, are you going to be okay if I leave soon? I'm taking my man home to continue the festivities behind closed doors."

"That's already too much information. Go on. Go be dirty with our old teacher."

She cackles. "You're so funny. I'll text you sometime tomorrow—probably after lunch—and we'll come back to tidy up." She kisses us both on the cheek and dances off.

"So, what do you say we head off soon, too, and conduct our own festivities behind closed doors?" Kurt suggests.

The very idea gives me butterflies. I can't wait to get the man naked. "I'm down with that. I'll just make sure everyone has a way of getting to wherever they're headed next."

Amy and Stacey assure me they'll be fine if we leave since they have an exclusive party in the Valley to attend soon. Jackson and Cash have invited

Rachel and Chris back to their place for more drinks and a game of Cards Against Humanity—so I wave goodbye to everyone, asking Amy to lock up behind her when she's ready.

Kurt and I stumble onto the street and begin the forty-five-minute walk home. We'd decided it would be easier to walk back to Kangaroo Point than find an Uber or cab on such a busy night. Besides, it's a great walk, mostly along the river. We catch the end of the fireworks as we pass the crowds of families camped out on picnic blankets—and listen to the music piped in along the esplanade through temporary speakers.

"Who would want to live anywhere else?" I say dreamily, using Kurt for balance.

"I know. It's a pretty great city. Do you ever miss Shell Beach?"

"You mean to live?"

"Yeah."

"I don't know. Maybe sometimes. But I love the convenience of Brisbane. Why? Do you?"

"I guess I was thinking about the future, and if I were to have a family. I'd like my kids to grow up on the coast."

I stop and face him. "*If* you were to have a family? What does that mean?"

He smiles. "I didn't want to put any pressure on you because you've never really talked about kids. I was just speaking hypothetically…"

"You want kids?" I mean, I know he said as much back in 1997, but I wasn't sure if he still felt that way.

He doesn't answer immediately, but after a pause, he says, "Yeah, I think I do."

More butterflies swarm in my belly. "And you want them with me?"

He reaches out and wraps both hands around my face so he's looking directly at me. "Yes. You are the only one I want them with."

I almost melt into a puddle right then and there. Is there anything sexier than a man saying he wants to father your children? But then the practicalities sink in. He's right. I haven't mentioned having children because I still haven't worked out if Ed is the reason I never had them, or if it was my own desire to stay childless.

"You know with me being over forty, it might not be easy to conceive?" I warn.

"I'm aware that nothing about being a parent is something to take lightly. But I'd like to try."

"Can I think about it?" I have to admit, the idea of having a couple of mini people who arise from a combination of mine and Kurt's DNA has crossed my mind more than once. I just never followed it through to a possible reality, mostly because we've only been together properly for eight months.

"Of course you can think about it. And I promise it's not a deal-breaker if you say no."

"Are you sure?"

He kisses me firmly on the mouth. "Yes, I'm sure. Now, come on. I want to get you home so we can do that thing that occasionally makes a baby, but in this case, won't."

I laugh. "I like your thinking."

We walk arm in arm over the bridge towards the cliffs near my apartment.

I have a lot to think about. But I'm not scared to face these decisions when Kurt is there beside me every step of the way.

Read the rest here: https://mybook.to/1998

BOOKS BY KIRSTY MCMANUS

My Own Personal Rockstar

https://mybook.to/MyOwnPersonalRockstar

Love at Coco Bay (Coco Bay Series Book #2)

https://mybook.to/LoveAtCocoBay

Welcome to Coco Bay (Coco Bay Series Book #1)

https://mybook.to/WelcomeToCocoBay

Before Coco Bay (A Coco Bay Series prologue)

https://mybook.to/BeforeCocoBay

A Christmas Rescue
(co-authored with Diane Michaels)

https://mybook.to/AChristmasRescue

Mind Reader

https://mybook.to/MindReader

I Thought It Was You

https://mybook.to/IThoughtItWasYou

1998 (90s Flashback Series Book #3)

https://mybook.to/1998

1997 (90s Flashback Series Book #2)

https://mybook.to/1997

1996 (90s Flashback Series Book #1)

https://mybook.to/1996

MultiDate

https://mybook.to/MultiDate

Lightweight

https://mybook.to/Lightweight

Perfume Therapy

https://mybook.to/PerfumeTherapy

How Not To Handle a Breakup

(formerly Saved by the Celebutante)

https://mybook.to/HowNotToHandleABreakup

Zen Queen

https://mybook.to/ZenQueen

ABOUT THE AUTHOR

Kirsty McManus was born in Sydney, Australia and moved to Queensland when she was 14. When she was 25, she lived in Japan for a year with her partner Kesh and worked as an English teacher. This was the inspiration behind her debut novel, *Zen Queen*. She also spent a year in Canada and then settled back down on the Sunshine Coast in 2008. Her writing often features characters visiting different countries and / or finding themselves in unusual situations. She is a little bit obsessed with vampires (Damon and Stefan are her favourites) and hopes to one day write her own epic vampire series.